FREEDOM AND THE TRAGIC LIFE

A STUDY IN DOSTOEVSKY

FREEDOM AND THE TRAGIC LIFE

A STUDY IN DOSTOEVSKY

by

VYACHESLAV IVANOV

Foreword by

Sir Maurice Bowra

THE NOONDAY PRESS

A DIVISION OF FARRAR, STRAUS
AND GIROUX

NEW YORK

Translated by

NORMAN CAMERON

Edited by

PROFESSOR S. KONOVALOV (Oxford)

Sixth printing, 1971

Library of Congress Catalog Card Number: 57-7979

MANUFACTURED IN THE UNITED STATES OF AMERICA
by The Murray Printing Company

Contents

ACKNOWLEDGMENT

The Publisher's thanks are due to Messrs. Heinemann Ltd. for permission to quote from their editions of Dostoevsky's *Crime and Punishment*, *The Idiot*, *The Possessed* and *The Brothers Karamazov*, translated by Constance Garnett.

Foreword

VYACHESLAV IVANOV. (1866-1949) possessed
to an unusual degree a remarkable accomplishment
both in scholarship and in poetry. As a young man he
studied under Mommsen, and his first published work
was a dissertation on taxation in the Roman Empire.
He absorbed all that was best in the German philological
training at a time when it was directed by men of genius,
and to this he owed not only his lasting love of the
antique world but his masterly knowledge of it. As a
poet, he was slow to mature and to publish, but when
he broke into print, it was clear that a new and powerful
talent had appeared. In the early years of this century
Ivanov established himself as a central figure of the
Russian Symbolists, who were giving new life to Russian
poetry after its long sloth in the 'eighties and 'nineties.
He encouraged others by his criticism and himself wrote
a powerful and original poetry, in which his vision of
Hellenism was united to his profound sense of the
Russian past. Never perhaps an easy poet, and at times
too hieratic for vulgar taste, he did not win fame quickly,
but now that we can see his work in its proper perspective
it is clear that it has qualities which outlast the years and
gain a new strength with them. Always an accomplished
and enterprising craftsman, he was no advocate of "art
for art's sake" but a mystical seer who sought to find
what was common to Hellenism and Christianity and to
form a new and living synthesis from the symbols and
myths of the European past. With advancing years he
wrote poetry more sparingly, especially after he left

Russia in 1922 and settled in Italy. But his later poetry has lost nothing in quality, even if it is simpler than his early work. He kept to the last a poet's outlook on life and was keenly aware of the need to maintain the great European heritage of imaginative creation. A man of great learning and generous culture, he was at home in several languages both living and dead, and though he had powerful convictions on both politics and religion, he never allowed them to spoil his art but made them conform to a mystical and philosophical outlook in which ideas of great range and scope were presented with clarity and decision. His book on Dostoevsky shows the strength of his convictions and the keenness of his insight. In Dostoevsky he saw someone akin to himself in his passionate devotion to the spiritual life and his vivid observation of the world around him. Ivanov was a great European, a Russian who possessed to a remarkable degree his countrymen's powerful interest in all matters that concern the human soul and yet tempered this by his love of all the great things which in three thousand years the West has given to the world.

C. M. BOWRA

Part I

Tragedic Aspect

Part I

Tragedic Aspect

Τραγῳδούμενα

MANY things have happened since Dostoevsky's death, yet his work and influence are more alive than ever before.

The creatures of his fantasy are instinct with a daemonic vitality. They do not retreat from us with the passage of time; they do not age; they refuse to withdraw into the ethereal regions of the Muses, there to become objects of our alien and dispassionate contemplation. From the fog in the streets they arise before us; in dark and sleepless nights they knock at our doors, frequent our bedsides and in confidential whispers engage us in many a disquieting conversation.

On the furthest horizon Dostoevsky has lit beacons of such radiant brilliance that they seem to us not terrestrial fires, but stars in heaven; but he, all the while, is at our sides, guiding their rays into our breasts— their cruelly healing lancets of light, more searing than molten steel. At every palpitation of our hearts, he says to us: "Yes, I know; and I know more, and much else besides." Amidst the roar of the maelstrom calling us, amidst the yawn of the chasm enticing us, rises the sound of his pipes, the sanity-destroying pipes of the deep. And inexorably he stands before us, with his penetrating,

3

enigmatic gaze, the sombre and keen-eyed guide through the labyrinth of our souls, simultaneously guiding us and spying upon us.

He dwells in our midst, and changes as we do; for, by dint of his steady concentration upon that which is universally and basically human; of his enormous psychological and ontological intensification and sharpening of the conflicts of his century; and also of the peculiar effects of the ferment he induced, which had the power to stir up all the depths of our conscious and subconscious existence—by dint of all these, he has certainly made a greater contribution than any other modern writer to the development of that intellectual and spiritual complexity which is the essential characteristic of present-day self-awareness. Just as Turner, according to the well-known saying, invented the London fog, so Dostoevsky discovered, revealed, and raised into reality the previously unrecognized multiplicity of fissures, strata and ambiguities in modern humanity—that is to say, everlasting humanity in its latest manifestation. He has asked the coming age questions that had never been asked before, and has whispered answers to questions not foreseen.

The origin of this mighty problematology, however, lies in his artist's intuition into the most secret motives, evasions, and recesses of the personality. Before him, nothing was known either of "The Man from Underground", nor yet of supermen of the type of Raskolnikov (in *Crime and Punishment*) or Kirillov (in *The Possessed*)—those self-supposed central focuses of the universe; glowing in the garrets and backyards of St. Petersburg; those fugitives from God and the world, around whom revolve, as around an axis, not only the social order that rejects them, but also the whole world that they themselves reject; those from whom, in their hidden nooks of refuge, the new-modelled Zarathustra learnt so much. Nobody before him had known that in those cavernous hearts there was room enough for the perpetual battle in the heavens between the spiritual legions of Michael and of Lucifer, contending for mastery of the world.

Eavesdropping upon destiny, Dostoevsky learnt the deepest secrets of human unity and human freedom: that life is basically tragic, because man is not what he is; that Paradise blooms around us here on earth, and we fail to see it only because we do not wish to do so; that the guilt of the individual is binding upon us all, just as his salvation saves us all, and his suffering makes atonement for us all; that the sinfulness of an evil deed may be cleansed away, because all must take it upon themselves—but not the sinfulness of an evil dream of the world, because the dreamer holds a mirror to himself in solitude, and must therefore continue his dream; that faith in God and denial of God are not simply two different conceptions of the world, but two essentially different worlds of the spirit, existing side by side, like an Earth and a counter-Earth, each fully living for itself in its own orbit of activity.

In order to explore, and give new depth to the world within us, and to disentangle the elements of our spiritual life, this new Daedalus had himself to be one of the most complex and powerful of artists. He was the master-builder of that subterranean labyrinth which was to give birth to the new spirituality of the universal, all-human Ego. That is why his poet's vision was steadily directed inwards; that is why one so seldom sees in his works the bright face of the earth, or the sun shining over green lawns—but only, now and then, the stars gleaming through cracks in the vault overhead: like the stars "of more than common size and splendour" that Dante saw at night, through the narrow mouth of a cavern of Purgatory.

> Poco potea parer li del di fuori,
> Ma per quel poco vedev' io le stelle
> Di lor solere a piu chiare e maggiori.

But the distance between cavern and star is far too great to be bridged by means of the pure epic, which is like a river spreading in gentle eddies over a flat plain. Only some unprecedentedly Dionysiac form of art could tell how chasms of the soul call to one another (*Abyssus abyssum invocat*—*Psalms* xli, 8). A stage-play would not be suited to this purpose, since neither is it introspective enough, nor able to show all the strata of human self-determination.

There was, however, a vehicle for such a composite creation, which, without being especially fit for a Dionysiac state of mind, was at least Protean—that is to say, so fluid and transmutable that it seemed bound to no set form, comprising, with equal readiness and flexibility, narration and commentary, dialogue and soliloquy, the telescopic and the microscopic, the dithyrambic and the analytical. Moreover, it prided itself on being the representative art-form of the present time, and even dared to challenge comparison with the great art-forms of the past. After all, why shouldn't the new chariot of Dionysus make its entry along the crowded highway of the novel?

Thus it is that the narrator of wanderings in the labyrinth, where his ecstatic worship of Mother Earth was for him Ariadne's thread, reveals himself unwittingly as a tragedian; and under his pen the novel becomes a tragedy in epic dress, like the *Iliad*.

Chapter I

THE NOVEL-TRAGEDY

I

WHAT strikes us at the first glance in Dostoevsky's work, is the very close approximation of the novel-form to the prototype of tragedy. It is not as if he had deliberately, and for artistic reasons, striven for this approximation. On the contrary, he arrived at it accidentally and in all simplicity. His whole being demanded it. He could create in no other way, because in no other way could he achieve either an intellectual conception or an artist's vision of life. The inner structure of his creative genius was tragic.

Thus it came about, entirely of itself, that whatever Dostoevsky had to express in his epic-narrative style (he never attempted to write a play: the limitations of the stage were obviously too narrow for him) was shaped—both in whole and in part, and of inward necessity—to conform with the laws of tragedy. His work is the most striking example we know of the identity of form and content—in so. far as by content we mean the original intuitive perception of life, and by form the means of transmuting this by art into the flesh and blood of a new world of living entities.

Aeschylus said of himself that his works were only

the crumbs from Homer's feast. The *Iliad* emerged, as the first and greatest of tragedies, at a time when there could be no question of tragedy as an art-form. Chronologically the oldest, and in its perfection the incomparable, monument of the European epic, the *Iliad* is essentially a tragedy as much in its general conception and in the development of its action, as in the pathos that informs it. According to an ancient definition, the *Iliad* is, in contradistinction to the "ethical" *Odyssey*, a "pathetic" poem—that is to say, a poem that portrays the sorrows and woes of its heroes. In the *Odyssey* the tragic tension which till then was the basic element of epic poetry has already been exhausted; and from this point onwards there begins a slow decline of the heroic epic in general.

The novel-form, on the other hand, has developed in a contrary direction. In modern times it has evolved with ever greater power and impact, becoming ever more many-sided and comprehensive, until finally, in its urge to acquire the characteristics of great art, it has become capable of conveying pure tragedy.

Plato described the epic as a hybrid, or mixed, form, partly narrative or instructive, partly mimetic or dramatic—the latter in those passages where the narration is interrupted with numerous and extensive monologues or dialogues, by the characters, whose words reach us in *oratio recta*, directly from the mouths of the masks that the poet has conjured into existence upon the imaginary tragic stage. Plato concludes that, on the one hand, lyrical or epic-lyrical enunciations (expressing what the poet says in his own person), and, on the other hand, the drama (comprising everything that the poet relates word for word as authentic sayings of his heroes) are two natural and clearly distinct forms

8

of poetry; whereas the epic combines in itself both lyrical and dramatic elements. This dual nature of the epic, as it was recognized by Plato, may be explained on the assumption that it arose from the conglomerate art of ancient times—the art described by Alexander Veselovsky, and defined by him as "syncretic"—in which the epic was not yet distinguished from ritual musical performances and imitative masked plays.[1] Be that as it may, the tragic element in the *Iliad*—its substance and internal form—is our historical reason for regarding the novel-tragedy not as a decadent form of the purely epic romance, but as an enrichment of it; as the reinstatement of the epic in the full inheritance of its rights. And what entitles us to apply the term "novel-tragedy" to the novels of Dostoevsky is, above all, their basic conception, which is thoroughly and essentially tragic.

"The joy of the story-teller"—the self-sufficing pleasure in invention of adventures and surprising entanglements, in the many-coloured tapestry of over-lapping and interlocking situations—at one time this was the novelist's professed main object. And it seemed that in this pleasure the epic narrator could find himself entirely anew: carefree, loquacious, inexhaustibly inventive, without any particular desire—or, indeed, real ability—to find the moral of his story. Always he remained loyal to his old predisposition to bring the tale to a happy ending: an ending that would fully satisfy the sympathies aroused in us by our continual partici-pation in the good and ill luck of the hero, and would bring us, after lengthy journeys on the flying carpet, back home to our customary surroundings—leaving us sated

---

[1] A survival of the rhythmical alternation of two interlocutors in the Homeric formula: Τὸν δ'ἀπομειβόμενος.

9

with the rich diversity of life mirrored in the bright phantasmagoria of the threshold between reality and dream, and at the same time filled with a healthy hunger for new experiences in our own existence.

The enchantment of this "idle musing" is, of course, irrevocably lost to our overclouded and restless epoch. Besides, some vigorous offshoots had branched away from the main stem of the post-medieval novel-literature: the humorous and satiric stories, the didactic or utopian narrative, and, last but not least, since Boccaccio's *Fiammetta*, the sentimental love-tale.

Nevertheless, the story-teller's art survived, and continued to exploit its flexible, accommodating technique, its own natural wealth of unexpected events, their puzzling complexities and the art of holding the reader in suspense as he awaits the unravelment of an apparently hopeless tangle: and all this Dostoevsky refused to renounce—as also did Balzac and Dickens, who notably influenced him—and he was right to do so. In his case, however, this motley material is subordinated to a special and higher architectural purpose: in all its component parts, however insignificant they may seem, it subserves the construction of a unified tragedy

In the circumstantial and seemingly exaggerated matter-of-factness of Dostoevsky's style no detail however small may be omitted: so closely do all particulars of the action cohere to the unity of the successive episodes of the story—separated though these are by numerous discursive passages. These episodes, in turn, are worked into the shape of acts, so to speak, in a continually unfolding drama; and these acts, finally, represent in their sequence the iron links of a chain of logic—on which, like a planetary body, hangs the main event which was from the beginning the theme and purpose of the whole work, with all the weight of its contentual and solemn significance; for in this planetary sphere Ormuzd and Ahriman have again matched themselves in battle, and the work has found its own Apocalypse, its own Day of Judgement.

2

In its whole plan, every novel by Dostoevsky is directed towards a tragic catastrophe. In one respect only does he depart from the poetical form of tragedy (we are speaking here not of the narrative, outer form, but solely of the inner structure of the story): namely, that at each moment we are confronted, not with a few simple outlines of an event, but with tragedy raised, so to speak, to a higher power. It is as if we saw the tragedy through a magnifying-glass, and found in its cell-structure a repetition and emphasis of the same principle of antinomy that informs the whole organism. Each cell carries within it the germ of an agonistic development; and, if the whole is catastrophic, so then is each synapse of the particular. This is the explanation of Dostoevsky's law of epic rhythm, which exactly accords with the essential nature of tragedy: the law of the progressively gathering momentum of events; the law that binds his works into a single system of taut nerves and muscles.

This characteristic is what gives these works a power over us that becomes all the greater with the degree of effort required by the ever steeper ascent. This fact, indeed—and not Dostoevsky's "vivisection of the living soul"—is the real reason for the frequent complaints about his "cruel talent". It is certainly true that, throughout the whole course of his narrative, which becomes more anxiously sombre at each turn of the road, Dostoevsky allows us no delight or enjoyment. Not even the exuberance of his humour, which, in romantic manner, he has lavishly spread throughout his work, can bring us any good cheer. We must drink the cup of bitterness to the dregs before we can be granted comfort and light in the "tragic purification".

But what, exactly, in Dostoevsky's writings, is this "purification", the mention of which in Aristotle's famous definition of tragedy has given rise to so many different interpretations?

The "catharsis" was the ideal scope of ancient tragedy. At a time when tragedy had not yet lost its religious significance, the catharsis was appropriately regarded as a comforting and beatifying boon of spiritual healing: devout participants in the Dionysiac passion-rite felt themselves, at the conclusion of the religious drama, absolved and sanctified. For Aristotle, on the other hand, who sought to establish an independent aesthetic free from religious admissions, the catharsis was a *medicina animae* in the psychological sense: a restoration of spiritual equilibrium, a liberation of the soul from the emotions stirred up by the tragedy (emotions whose forces, as long as they find no outlet, accumulate dangerously in men's bosoms, but can be beneficially "unloaded" in the course of an imaginary participation in some tragic fate), and especially from the emotions of fear and pity.

It must not be forgotten, of course, that we are now considering a theoretical structure, whose creator had no personal experience of Greek tragedy in its prime. Aristotle himself states, significantly enough, that it is better to read a tragedy than to see it on the stage. It was therefore natural that he should secularize the traditional notions of Dionysiac purification, Dionysiac conquest of the fear of death, and Dionysiac compassion for the suffering hero, in order, by a shrewd re-interpretation, to preserve them for secular culture.

Fear and tormenting pity—exactly according to the Aristotelian formula—are just what Dostoevsky's Muse evokes. She is a "cruel" Muse, because she is to the last degree tragic; but she always leads us to an uplifting and liberating final convulsion of the spirit: thereby revealing the authenticity and purity of her art, for which it would be hard to find a more accurate epithet than "purifying", whether we choose to regard the much-disputed concept of catharsis under its psychological, metaphysical or moral aspect.

Direct experience tells us, as soon as we have traversed a great work by this epic poet-tragedian, that our tender hearts have not been stung in vain; that some inerasable mark has been left upon us; that we have become somehow different; that, indeed, a quite inconceivable and nevertheless joyful confirmation of the meaning and value of life and suffering has begun to shine like a star in our souls, which have been ennobled by the secret sacrifice of a shared renunciation, and blessed and redeemed by the painful gift of a spiritual parturition.

This is the effect that the author sought to achieve. Just as the dramatists of ancient times wrote particular plays—*Prometheus Unbound*, *The Eumenides* and *Oedipus Coloneus*, for example—whose object was to set a solemn seal upon the expiatory apotheosis of heroic suffering; so Dostoevsky depicts for us, in the epilogue to *Crime and Punishment*, the spiritual revival of a man who is inherently good, but has gone darkly astray—a revival like that of a young shoot sprouting vigorously from healthy roots when the withered old trunk has been burnt to ashes by the thunderbolt of wrath. Similarly, the final section of *The Brothers Karamazov* contains such a sublime glorification of the heroic child-martyr that we are entirely consoled, and bless his obscure sacrifice as a source of immeasurable comfort. So creatively powerful, so illuminating are the consolation and new strength bestowed by the author upon the soul that has followed him through all the torments of Hell and the pains of Purgatory, that we have long since become reconciled to our stern guide and have ceased to complain of the rigours of the journey.

It is foolish to condemn as an artistic imperfection anything that leads to such a result. One may, however, discover a fault of literary style in the monotony of certain devices that Dostoevsky uses, which seem like a direct application of stage technique to epic narrative: the artificial juxtaposition, for example, of characters and events in the same place and time; dialogues that might be impressive behind the footlights, but are not true to life; likewise the presentation of every physical development in the form of catastrophic shocks, in passionate confessions and public disclosures made in circumstances that, although effective on the stage, lack all verisimilitude; the rounding-off of individual scenes by sheer *coups de théâtre*; and lastly—at moments when the catastrophe has not yet matured and therefore cannot yet be enacted—its anticipation in scenes of brawl and uproar.

3

Since Dostoevsky's artistic conventions—which are likewise predominantly those of the stage, and to which he adheres strictly—demand that every spiritual development shall reveal itself in action, he seeks, under the guidance of his tragic view of life, to express the basic antinomy of tragedy in antinomic action. This is invariably presented as an infringement: an infringement—according as we choose to regard it—either upon the cosmic order (compare the divine tragedy of the ancients, dealing with the guilt of a Prometheus, a Pentheus or a Hippolytus), or upon the rules of society (compare *Antigone*); in which latter case the most aggravated form of infringement is what we call crime.

Crime, therefore, becomes the centre of Dostoevsky's tragic world; and in his exhausting analysis of it he sets himself to examine and demonstrate all that he has learnt of the most secret motives of human desire and endeavour. This analysis must, of course, be primarily either psychological or sociological; but this great psychologist—who nevertheless opposes to psychological study a "more real" penetration into the secret of human nature—cannot rest here. His own most private experience has led him, in his fathoming of the depths of the human heart, far beyond what is empirically definable or definite; and it is just this insight into the supra-empirical nature of free will that sets the stamp of tragedy upon his primitive intuition of life. Not in the earthly stage of being lie the roots of that intellectual and spiritual substance, clothed in flesh, which is known as man, but in an existence beyond this world; and each individual destiny has its "Prologue in Heaven". In that transcendent sphere where God and Devil do battle over the fate of the creature—and "their battlefield is in the hearts of men"—here *incipit tragoedia*.

For man, when empirically considered, appears to be, if not entirely without freedom, yet certainly not absolutely free. But this is not so; for, if it were, then man could not be man—that is to say, he would not be the only one of God's creatures to experience life tragically. However much he may depend, both in his material and also in his spiritual existence, upon the external world, he bears within his inmost core his own autonomous law, to which all his environment somehow, like a plastic stuff, adapts itself. The ultimate principle of his reaction to the world and his action upon it—the insoluble content of his Ego—is determined from within, and maintains itself essentially independent. Moreover—since the word "tragic" can be used but improperly so long as there is no free self-determination—the true tragedy of a human life is perceptible in external manifestations only in so far as these reflect the extra-temporal and original tragedy of the "intelligible character" (in Kant's acceptation of this term). Thus it comes about that Dostoevsky sets the real key-point of the tragic tangle in the realm of metaphysics; for only here we are allowed to premise the pure activity of the free will and have an insight into it through the prism of art.

Dostoevsky is thus obliged to give a threefold explanation for crime. Firstly he has to settle the metaphysical act of the individual will—which, in the conflict of being-in-itself and being-in-God, must either choose between the two or, at least, subordinate one to the other, thus freely determining the fundamental law of its existence. Secondly, he has to explore the psychological pragmatism—that is to say, the connection between, and development of, the peripheral conditions of consciousness, the linking together of experience, the pathology of the passions, the ebb and flow of emotional stimuli—all of which lead to the final step, and induce the final emotion necessary to the committing of the crime.

Thirdly and lastly, he has to investigate the pragmatism of external events, the whole net of apparently accidental occurrences, fine as a cobweb, yet ever thickening its mesh until it is unbreakable, the net that life casts about the victim, the chain of actions and combination of circumstances whose causality inescapably conduces to the crime. The joint effect of all these factors, moreover, is brought into relation with processes occurring in the social sphere; so that we can clearly understand how the collective will, too, secretly plays a part in the individual will's act of self-determination.

Thus this *maestro di color che sanno*—a master amongst those who know the human heart—succeeds, by his threefold exploration of the causes of the crime, in laying bare the most deeply hidden tragedy contained in the dualism of necessity and free will as components of human destiny. He leads us, so to speak, to the loom of life, and shows us how the threads of both intersect and are enmeshed together at every crossing of warp and woof. His metaphysical interpretation of events is implicit in his psycho-empirical interpretation. The main direction of the path that each individual takes is laid down for him by his inmost will—whether resting in God or opposing itself to God; and it seems, indeed, that whereas the outer and superficial volition and endeavour are subject in all particulars to the law of life, yet this latter is passive before a higher determining agency, willed by man himself, which in fact is the expression of his free self-determination. For this fundamental decision, whether to be for God or against Him, is unceasingly expressed in man's conscious self-subjection to the imperative guidance of countless spirits, which order him to tread just here and not there, to do just this and not that.

Indeed, once the metaphysical choice has been made, there is for each individual only one possible course of action. Self-opposition is no longer practicable; and the decision, once taken, is unalterable, because it is sustained by the whole substance of the human Ego, which in its choice has determined its own nature and fate.

Thus what in Sophoclean tragedy appears as an inscrutable decree of destiny is exalted by Dostoevsky (as also by Aeschylus, who does not admit *Ananke* and attributes the tragic issue to an ancestral doom) to a supra-conscious act of will by the human soul, which either turns towards God—and thus, for the length of its earthly life, retains deep within itself an awareness of Him and belief in Him; or turns away from Him—and can then, all its life long, no more remember Him or believe in Him, even if it yearns for Faith or speaks of Faith. Hovering solitary in the void, such a soul finds no true access to men—for only in God can man truly be known by man. It dreams of mankind and of the world, and hates both the dream and its own yearning for the tormenting dream's deception. It would slay the shadows that swarm around it, and desperately seeks, by plunging into non-existence, to rid itself of the incubus oppressing it.

Only a hallowed spiritual death, followed by rebirth—the death of the "old man" within the personality— might still save this soul, giving it salvation by the offered boon of chastisement. But this death and rebirth, which we have compared to the putting-forth of a new shoot from healthy roots, can take place only if the roots are, in fact, healthy—that is to say, if the defection from God has not been the result of a final decision by the metaphysical Ego, but has signified only an antithetical impulse in the supra-conscious drama—the impulse of wilful self-alienation from God which comes of arrogance and a desire for unbridled exercise of the self; the impulse of voluntary withdrawal and self-waste (a sort of κένωσις of mankind's god-like qualities). After the bitter experiences and disappointments that such an impulse produces, after all the errors and crimes to which it leads, there is still always the possibility of return to the Father's House, still always the *Domine, memento mei* of the repentant evil-doer.

4

It must be added, however, that Dostoevsky's urge at any cost to reveal innermost states of the soul through manifestations resembling those of stagecraft has, in its turn, a damaging effect upon his epical calm and clarity. The over-emphasis inherent in this mode of presentation conveys an impression of morbidity, even where the experience depicted, however confused it may be, is in itself in no way morbid. The pathetic element is carried to a point at which it threatens to deteriorate into over-excitement, or even into hysteria. Those characters in the novel who most deeply suffer from the tragic dichotomy, act and behave as if in a continual state of alternately calm and turbulent ecstasy.

In sharp contrast to the over-excited tone of the conversations, the style of the narrative is businesslike and sober, reminiscent of a court of law; and, when the whole novel is a study in criminology, the reader often feels as if he were present at a distressing, prolonged and extremely complicated trial. One must, however, pay this price for the enjoyment—painful, yet so uniquely deep and moving—that one derives from the magnificent works of this singular genius.

By means of an extremely detailed and matter-of-fact reportage, the author creates the illusion of a strictly realistic depiction of actual events; of an absolute and almost documentary reliability. Thus he disguises the purely poetic and ideal nature—powerfully soaring high above the empirical—of the world that he has conjured into being: a world which is not the same as that of our day-to-day experience, but which so truthfully reflects the latter's secret meaning and development, and is seen with such clairvoyance in its relation to actual life, that reality itself seems to hasten to respond, to this Columbus of the human heart, with a disclosure of all the vistas that he has foreseen—and, one might almost think, foreordained—vistas that have never before risen above the horizon.

Whilst the illusion of a complete accordance with the rhythm and perspective of reality blinds the reader to the almost dangerous dimensions of this Russian Shakespeare's uninhibited fantasy, yet, on the other hand, behind the deliberately prosaic and official-seeming style, scorning all rhetorical embellishment, is concealed the trenchancy and graphic force of a mode of speech that is uniquely expressive and equal to the demands of its subject: a mode of speech that, if only for its liberating vigour, its assault upon all the established airs-and-graces of literature, upon all smooth affectation and falsity, is of immeasurable value.

Dostoevsky has, however, yet another sort of especial grasp of his medium, which enables him to turn his police-court records, as if by a miracle, into poetry: he has a masterly understanding of how to enhance the tragic atmosphere of the whole work by effects of illumination, by contrasts and gradations of light and shade. In this respect he resembles Rembrandt, whose characterization by Baudelaire vividly reminds one of Dostoevsky's doleful realms—for instance, of his *House of the Dead*:

> Rembrandt, triste hôpital, tout rempli de murmures
>   Et d'un grand crucifix décoré seulement,
> Où la prière en pleurs s'exhale des ordures,
>   Et d'un rayon d'hiver traversé brusquement.

In the works of Tolstoy, Dostoevsky's great contemporary and rival, everything is bathed in a diffused light that prevents us from becoming so absorbed in the particular as completely to forget the vast surrounding areas of the whole. In Dostoevsky's works, on the contrary, dark shadows fall, one upon the other, in the corners of gloomy dungeons; whilst a deliberately contrived illumination is glimmeringly refracted upon the vaults and around the recesses. Just so must the labyrinth appear to him who explores the casemates of the spirit, causing the light of his torch to fall upon hundreds of faces that flicker before its flickering flame—faces into whose eyes he gazes with his grave, searching, penetrating gaze.

For Dostoevsky, the watcher and spy upon the occult depths of our souls, needs no daylight. On purpose he veils his poetic creations in half-darkness; so that, like the ancient Furies, he may steal by night upon the culprit, catch him hidden behind a ledge of rock, and then suddenly shed a lurid glare upon the pale and swooning murderer, staring involuntarily at the motionless and blood-drenched body of his victim.

Dostoevsky's Muse resembles, in her ecstatic nature and power of divination, the Dionysiac Maenad, possessed by her god, who "with loudly beating heart (παλλομένη κραδίην) follows her wild career"; and she also resembles that other manifestation of this Maenad—the snake-haired daughter of darkness, the bloodhound-bitch of the Goddess of Night, the avenging Fury—acquainted with destiny, inexorable and un-resting—carrying a torch in one hand, and a scourge of serpents in the other.

Chapter II

THE TRAGIC PRINCIPLE IN
DOSTOEVSKY'S PHILOSOPHY OF LIFE

I

THE expression "naïve idealism" may well be applied to that primitive perception of life which seems to be connatural to man as an individual, and whose spell makes him take the surrounding reality for a part of his own *Ego* just awakened to self-awareness: at this stage the real meaning of the *Tu* is yet unknown.

The evolution of family and community, and the discovery of the forces mysteriously working from without in the world form a transition (marked by the development of ritual, judicial and ethical laws) to the age of "naïve realism".

This soil is fertile enough to produce the germination of higher morality, firmly rooted in religion, which strengthens the bonds connecting man with the beings above and underneath and around him; whilst the gradual decay of ancient belief once more urges him, though now on the way of reflection, towards the pole of his innate idealism.

Because, however, this idealism has long since lost its original *naïveté*, the thinking Ego henceforth endeavours to sever the act of cognition from the empirical personality; and the subjective consciousness desires to universalize itself *in abstracto*, by means of pure thought.

The first, and probably the only, attempt to create a moral religion derived from idealistic conception, was Buddhism, which nowadays still exercises a strong attraction upon many natures. The spiritual outlook of the present time, however, has been chiefly conditioned by a school of thought that reached its culmination in Hegel—even though it occasionally (as in the writings of Feuerbach or Karl Marx) pays homage to the materialistic interpretation of nature.

At this point there arises, from the ruins of the great idealistic systems, a danger that ever since the second half of the last century has been making itself terrifyingly apparent—a danger in which Dostoevsky discovered one of the main matters of the immemorial human dispute with God.

It is true that, by practical experience acquired over thousands of years, man has been thoroughly taught not to adopt an independent attitude towards the world about him. Nevertheless, in the act of cognition—which after all, is the criterion of everything—he comes to know all things as objects wrought by himself. If, therefore, he has to seek the measure of things in himself, he is exposed to the temptation to regard himself as the sole creator of all standards. As soon as the Absolute has passed through the phase of being a metaphysical abstraction, and has become a mere conceptualistic phantom, the human understanding is irresistibly impelled to proclaim, as its final conclusion, that all accepted values are universally relative.

In these circumstances, it is no wonder if the personality, imprisoned in a subjectivist solitude, either yields itself to despair or falls a victim to the vainglorious delusion that it is dependent upon nothing. This is the danger that Dostoevsky has in mind when he writes, in the epilogue to *Crime and Punishment*, concerning a "new, unprecedented, terrible pestilence", which "is spreading over Europe from the depths of Asia".

Here is a passage:

Never before had men thought themselves so clever, never before had they believed so unshakably in their own wisdom, as did these sick creatures. Never before had men been so deeply convinced of the infallibility of their judgments, doctrines and principles. Whole districts, whole cities, whole nations caught the infection, and behaved like madmen. Everybody was in a state of high excitement, and nobody understood anyone else. Each man thought that he alone was in possession of the truth, and was deeply distressed—beating his breast, weeping and wringing his hands—at the sight of his fellows. Nobody knew on whom judgment should be passed, or what sort of judgment it should be; no two people could agree as to what was good or what was bad—who should be prosecuted or who should be acquitted. Men killed each other in a senseless fury. They marched to battle in great armies; but, before they had reached the battlefield, each army began to make war amidst itself; ranks were broken, and the warriors fell upon each other, stabbing and slashing, biting and devouring. In the cities alarm-signals were being given all day long; everyone answered summonses to mass-meetings—but who had summoned them, and for what purpose, nobody knew. Ordinary trades were abandoned, because everybody had his own suggestions for improving them, and no two people could agree. Agriculture was at a standstill.

In the whole world only a few people could save themselves. These were the pure elect, chosen to found a new human race, to create a new life, to renew and purify the world. But nobody noticed these people; nobody listened to their words, or even heard their voices.

This is how the redeemed Raskolnikov, when "already convalescent", remembered his delirium. But the symbolism of his dreaming soul merely reflected, in the enlarged dimensions of phantasy, the mad dream that he himself had dreamt, not long since, while wide awake: the mad dream of asserting himself as a superman within that state—we shall not say "of autarky", but, with greater significance, "of autarchy"—that state of solitary thinking and willing in which the whole world seems merely a plastic object of the one and only subject endowed with the magical power of cognition.

In opposition to the spiritual trend that has fostered such poisonous growths, Dostoevsky comes forward as the champion of a way of thought which he himself regards, not only as "realistic", but actually as realistic "in a higher sense". What, then, is the nature of this realism that he advocates?

2

Clearly this mode of thought is not based upon theoretical cognition, with its constant antithesis of subject and object, but upon an act of will and faith approximately corresponding to the Augustinian *transcende te ipsum*. Dostoevsky has coined for this a word of his own: *proniknovenie*, which properly means "intuitive seeing through" or "spiritual penetration". He has given this word almost the character of a *terminus technicus*.

It is a transcension of the subject. In this state of mind we recognize the other Ego not as our object, but as another subject. It is therefore not a mere peripheral extension of the bounds of individual consciousness, but a complete inversion of its normal system of coordinates.

The authenticity of this transvaluation is demonstrated primarily in one's inner life: in the experience of true love (which is the only real cognition, for the very reason that it is bound up with absolute faith in the reality of the beloved); and, more generally, in the self-surrender or self-renunciation with which the pathos of love is informed.

The spiritual penetration finds its expression in the unconditional acceptance with our full will and thought of the other-existence—in "Thou art". If this acceptance of the other-existence is complete; if, with and in this acceptance, the whole substance of my own existence is rendered null and void (*exinanitio*, κένωσις), then the other-existence ceases to be an alien "Thou"; instead, the "Thou" becomes another description of my "Ego". "Thou art" then no longer means "Thou art recognized by me as existing", but "I experience thy existence as my own, and in thy existence I again find myself existing". *Es, ergo sum.*

Certainly, altruism as a moral principle does not contain the totality of this experience, which is consummated in the mystic depths of the consciousness, in relation to which any standard of moral obligation becomes a subtraction.

Since, therefore, such a spiritual penetration is clearly outside the realm of intellectual cognition, Dostoevsky quite logically assigns it to the instinctively-creative life-principle, which he ranks over the principle of reason. At a time when—just as in the days of the Sophists—the notion of the relativity of spiritual values was beginning to infiltrate the mart of opinion, Dostoevsky, in contrast with Tolstoy, made no attempt to follow Socrates in the search for a criterion of "the good" which would accord with true knowledge. Like the ancient Greek dramatists, he remained true to the spirit of Dionysus. He would not accept the optimistic view that "the good" could be demonstrated by proofs, or that right knowledge alone could make mankind good. On the contrary, wholly inspired by Dionysus, he repeatedly proclaims: "Seek ye exaltation and ecstasy; kiss the earth, and learn from it that each is responsible for all, and shares in all guilt. In the joy of this exaltation and this understanding, ye shall find redemption. Verily, only so shall ye be made whole."

3

Realism in this sense means, above all, a peculiar attitude of the will, a qualitatively determined structure of its tension; which, however, also implies a particular sort of cognition. In so far as the will-to-good is aware of its own existence, it discovers in itself this essential power of cognition: we call it Faith.

Faith is a sign of the good health of the will. It sinks its earthly roots into the elementally-creative soil of life. In all its movements and urges, in its steady thrust and gravitation, it is as infallible as instinct:

> Good shepherds, lead us to life's cooling streams;
> Lead us, eternal guides, amidst the light
> Of suns invisible, beneath whose gleams
> The heart, in answer, blossoms in the night.[1]

Dostoevsky's realism was his faith, which he received after he had lost his "soul"—that is to say, his self-hood. His self-transposition into the other-Ego, his experience of the other-Ego as an original, infinite, freely autonomous world, contains in itself the postulate of God as a reality—more real than all the ontologically essential beings to each of whom, with all his will and all his conviction, Dostoevsky called out "Thou art". And this same self-transposition into the other-Ego, which is an

[1] Vyacheslav Ivanov.

act of the love that seeks to unite all men *ut |sint unum*
(*St. John* xvii, 23), of the love that strives to draw the
venom from the serpent's fangs of the *principium in-
dividuationis*, and calls death itself into the lists; this
self-transposition, which is at once the terror and the
bliss of the portentous realization that each is responsible
for all, and shares all guilt; this self-transposition contains
in itself also the postulate of Christ, who won the
redeeming victory over a world torn to pieces by
internecine strife and sunk in sin and death.

For, were there no *Ens Realissimum* and no Saviour,
then every effort of the personality to emerge from its
metaphysical solitude would be condemned in advance
to frustration and futility. But it is not so, however
ineffectual the effort of the individual may prove to be;
however little his "self-transposition" may be worth in
practice; what though the arrow of desire fail to reach
the very heart of its quarry—yet the effort can never
be false, or fundamentally mistaken:

> That which the inward voice doth say
> Ne'er leads the searching soul astray.[1]

Dostoevsky emphatically repeats Schiller's words:
"The heart's glow is Heaven's pledge." A pledge of
what? A pledge of the possibility of a complete vindication of man's yearning for deliverance from the
fetters forged by Original Sin—the fetters of alienation
from God and separation from one's neighbour: a
vindication of man's yearning for absolute oneness with
God. Thus can man apprehend God within himself:
"Either my heart lies, or God the Son of Man is truth.
He alone assures me of the reality of my realism, of the

---

[1]Schiller.

actuality of my actions. He alone makes real that which, in darkling awareness, I perceive to be the essence of myself and of the world."

Such a view, and such a personal experience of the other-Ego, lead Dostoevsky logically to the constantly reiterated assertion that men, those children of God, must inevitably destroy themselves and one another unless they recognize, in Heaven, the One Father, and, in their own brotherhood, Christ the Son of Man. If they fail to do this, then the realism founded on "Thou art" collapses; indeed, it turns into the opposite—a solipsistic nihilism.

For if, even after my attempt to transpose myself into the other-Ego, I still find within me no faith in God, then I say to myself: "It is evident that my loving fondness has deceived me: it did not, after all, contain the essential cognition that was to reveal to me the true Being. Furthermore, it clearly cannot have been true love; for, even as I said to my neighbour 'Thou art', I said in my heart 'In truth Thou art not'. To be sure, I felt myself entitled to exclaim: 'I experience thy existence as my own.' But, since I did not dare to add 'and through thy existence I again find myself existing', therefore the first part of my assertion was illusory and of no account; for all it meant was that both of us hover in the void, and are equally without substance. It would be vain, therefore, for the taut bow of my will any longer to wing the arrow of desire towards the other-Ego: again and again it returns upon me, and pierces my own bosom, after circling in an empty space which contains nothing more real than my own Ego, that insubstantial shadow of a dream."

Thereupon my love turns into hatred—for love can exist only in the world of reality, whereas hatred can blaze in a world of illusion. It is all one to me *whom* I hate: my fellow-men, those shadows that encompass me and resemble me—existing only in my perceptions, instead of holding me fast within reality and bringing me salvation; or myself, who exist in them as the phenomena of my dream. In any case, I may behave towards them as I please—after all, there is no constraint upon dreams—unless, indeed, I prefer to put an end to the evil dream, by killing myself and, with myself, the whole world contained within me.

Where atheism has been elevated to the practical norm of social existence, Dostoevsky holds that this entails first of all a deterioration and corruption of the moral sense, and subsequently its complete extinction. For morality not founded on religion is not capable, in the long run, of maintaining even the independence, much less the absoluteness, of its own values.

The stage of deterioration at which human dignity and freedom are no longer respected is described in *The Story of the Grand Inquisitor*. In this the shrewdest and boldest of men—men who feel themselves to be benefactors of the human race, which they thoroughly despise, and are inwardly proud of their own selflessness—exercise an unchecked tyranny over the human herd that provides them with food and physical comforts: the herd whose only consolation is its ignorance of the fact that it has been betrayed. And the end of it all is: cannibalism.

This train of thought leads to the conclusion that faith in God resembles a golden treasure, whose ready availability guarantees the value of the personality. If the treasure is exhausted, the personality is valueless. A few nobler natures cannot endure this ontological devaluation—accepted though it be by the *consensus omnium*—and either go mad or resort, in half-madness, to suicide, which they come to regard as the only action worthy of them. Such a one was Dostoevsky's young author of the *Letter from a Suicide*, which explains the latter's act as a protest against "Nature".

4

Thus the choice between "Yes" and "No"—the two answers that can be given to the transcendent, personal existence of God—is for Dostoevsky the same thing as the alternative: "To be or not to be." The personality, the goodness, the humanity; and, mystically comprising and conceptually compassing these, the Son of Man—all, in Dostoevsky's view, necessary corollaries of faith in the living God—do they exist, or did Christ die in vain? We must choose, that is to say, between the Christian justification—as the only possible one—of life and suffering, of man and of God Himself; and a metaphysical tumult, a plunge into the daemonic, a blind collapse into the abyss where Not-being labours, with terrifying pangs, to give birth to a being, and then devours its phantom progeny.

For, as soon as the human soul despairs of God, it is irresistibly drawn to chaos: it finds joy in all that is ugly and warped, and is greeted, from the deepest ravines of Sodom, by the smile of a beauty that seeks to rival the beauty of Our Lady.

The question of Faith thus becomes essentially the question of spiritual salvation. Only the redeeming and healing suffering can save man's ontological substance, his divine mission, from a mystical suicide.

Tolstoy, too, stood for a while, shuddering and despondent, at the parting of the ways where man makes the fateful choice. But, in his case, his great psychological need was to keep alive the value of individual existence; to preserve it against lurking satiety and disgust, by means of a eudaemonistic system of ethics. In this he succeeded, within the limits he set himself; for it was precisely because of his own increasing *taedium vitae* that he was, in the Buddhist sense (and in religion he scarcely sought for any other), already ripe for redemption.

Proceeding from his experience of the deep content that follows upon the performance of a moral act, Tolstoy defines the conditions whose fulfilment alone can give man the possibility of a lasting peace with himself and with God, with his fellow-men and with Nature:

> I am. My existence rests on the validity of truth and justice, on the foundations of reason and conscience, which are in such harmony that the demands of the latter are entirely ratified by the former—yea, that goodness and truth ultimately prove to be one. My existence becomes the true existence when this harmony stays undisturbed in my consciousness and fully and completely determines all expressions of my personality. I recognize the origin of this harmony within myself to be the breath of God; therefore I also have the certainty of God's existence, which is apart from my existence, yet conditions and determines it. The Divine Principle that resides within me is, of necessity, immortal.

This was the path that Tolstoy followed in his search for the *summum bonum*. To Dostoevsky's essentially tragic mind, however, this reassuring train of thought was alien. Indeed, it never completely reassured its own originator. In his criticism of Tolstoy's novel *Anna Karenina*, in which the hero follows just this track, and rejoices to find himself finally convinced of God's existence, Dostoevsky wonders whether what the hero has experienced is really Faith.

The growth of Dostoevsky's religious philosophy was not a slow ripening; still less a search directed from its outset towards definite ends, reaching its final result by stages, as knowledge advances by the interconnection of links of logic. It is true that Dostoevsky's work gives evidence of violent spiritual struggles, which provide this mighty dialectician with abundant material for the creation of those tragedies of the spirit in which the metaphysical tumult proclaims itself in many a different guise; but these gigantically sprouting antitheses are so balanced that—far from effacing the basic knowledge already won, and branded on the soul—they actually widen and deepen it.

The spiritual development of Dostoevsky's passionate personality is, therefore, not a gradual process of growth: on the contrary, the preoccupation with catastrophe which characterizes his works—as an effluence of their inherent tragedy—reveals itself also in his private life. It may be that during those moments when, at the place of execution, Dostoevsky looked into the eyes of death, he underwent a sudden and decisive transformation of the soul—a beatified death, followed by the unexpected gift of divine mercy to his corporeal shell. The years of forced labour and exile—spent in humility and renunciation by this former free-thinker and revolutionary, who now gave himself up to a fervent and loving study of the Gospels, and shared without resentment in the expiation of common malefactors—were for his inner personality the "youthful veil" in which he "hid himself": the swaddling bands tightly swathed about the new-born child, bringing about that extinction of his outer personality, of his stubborn self-consciousness, which was needed to consummate his resurrection.

At the place of execution, in those moments of

preparedness for death (which he later recalled in *The Idiot* and elsewhere), he felt that his soul had overrun death, and knew itself to be alive: living, indeed, more intensely than ever before (so great was the effort of will for which it had collected itself, in order not to shed any of its hitherto unsuspected vital power), in a life already beyond the threshold of the grave.

The personality was thus forcibly extricated from the conditions of its earlier existence, and became for the first time conscious of its own true substance, revealed behind the receding vision of external things, behind the wrappings falling from the embodied spirit. Like a midwife (for such experiences can be described only in images), that hour seems to have brought forth from limbo the inner-Ego slumbering in the depths of the soul's being—yet without cutting all the bonds that fastened it to the womb: for, indeed, a complete severance would mean death.

The life thus spared was, from that time onwards, a life of a singular character, not unlike the philosophic death extolled by Plato: a life whose summits towered high above the floods of life's ocean surging below; a life reaching up into a more spiritual, new element.

It seems as though, from that time onwards, Dostoevsky's consciousness had a different centre of gravity from that of most mortals. His outer man remained unaltered: one could not detect any thorough purging away of the dark passions concealed within it. But all the spiritual doing and striving of Dostoevsky were henceforth sustained by the inspiration of the newly created man within; for whom much that we regard as transcendent came to be in some way immanent in his being—just as, conversely, some part of what is given to us directly was for him now removed to an exterior region. His personality was, in fact, divided into an empirical entity and another, higher and more free, which was essentially metaphysical.

In most mystics this dichotomy produces either complete exhaustion or a deep purification and transfiguration of the outer man. But this act of sanctification was not to fall within the lot of a prophet whose task was that of an artist.

Not only did Dostoevsky give his double, who faced the outer world, full freedom to live as he chose, or as he was compelled, to live: we actually find the artist ever busy creating new doubles for himself, all of them contained behind the polymorphous masks of his own many-faced and all-human Ego, which is no more bound to *one* face. For the more the inner Ego is freed from the outer, the more closely it feels itself allied to all humanity; since, in the boundless wealth of individual differences, it recognizes only variously conditioned forms of its own subjection to the law of separate existence. The expression: "Nothing that is human is foreign to me" becomes a complete truth only when a new Ego, freed from all taint of human limitations, is brought to birth.

The foregoing is the reason why all Dostoevsky's revelations concerning the evil effect of spiritual isolation, or concerning that miracle of communion with the other-Ego which is achieved through the self-surrender of personality and its self-recovery in the œcumenical consciousness; concerning the real oneness of the human race, each individual's share in the guilt of the sins of others, and likewise his share in the fruits of a sanctity beyond his knowledge; concerning the Eleusinian mystery of our piously loving Mother Earth, her power of silent union and reconciliation, her acquaintance with death and resurrection, and (again to quote Schiller) "the believer's eternal covenant with her"; concerning "the touch of worlds more exalted" and their "seeds that God has sown here below"; concerning the ontological virtue of sheer joy in existence; concerning the definition of Hell's torment as an inability to love, etc., etc.: all these partially enigmatic-seeming declarations, admonitions and promises are simply attempts to impart to the world—if only by obscure hints—a knowledge of what was disclosed to Dostoevsky in the spiritual illumination of a horrifying experience, and thereafter, at intervals, came to life in his ecstatic premonitions of the ineffable "universal harmony". These premonitions, incidentally, were unmistakable precursors of Dostoevsky's attacks of epilepsy—that disease, accounted holy by the ancients, which seems to possess the power of obliterating the boundaries between "idealism" and "realism"; so that at moments the outer world becomes the inner, whilst conversely the inner world becomes alien and remote, and seems like a miraculous drama in the distance.

5

Thus it was by way of inward experience that Dostoevsky arrived at the discovery of the distinction between the empiric and the intelligible character: a distinction that Kant and Schopenhauer have demonstrated in philosophy. All Dostoevsky's observations on the nature of crime tacitly presuppose this distinction. It implies ontological postulates which were necessary to the explorer of "all the depths of the human soul", if he was "to find man in man".[1] In his creative presentation

---

[1]"Whilst keeping faith with realism (in art), to find man in man! . . . People call me a psychologist: this is inaccurate. I am a realist in the higher sense: that is to say, I indicate all the depths of the human soul."—*From Dostoevsky's Diary.*

of characters in their entirety, this distinction is enforced more clearly than in the works of almost any other author. And it is just this distinction which in Dostoevsky's novels invests his depictions of spiritual experience with a ghastly chiaroscuro reminiscent of Dante; with so incisive a penetration and so massive an effectiveness.

Dostoevsky presents each individual destiny as a single, coherent event taking place simultaneously on three different levels. The intricacy of his story-teller's dealings with actuality, the multifold composition of the texture of the plot, is in some sort the basis of a still greater complexity on the psychological plane.

On the two lower levels is displayed the whole labyrinthine diversity of life; and also the cunning of chance, which not seldom seems to have some secret understanding with the spirits who observe events on the uppermost, or metaphysical, level. On the lower levels is also revealed the changeability of the empirical character even within the bounds of its determination from without.

On the uppermost, or metaphysical, level, on the other hand, there is no more complexity or subjection to circumstance: here reigns the great, bare simplicity of the final—or, since here time has, in a sense, stood still, the first—decision, to which all that has come to pass can be traced, and from which, likewise, gushes all that is to be. Here we are granted an insight into man's innermost region—or, to use the author's own words, into "his heart as the field in which God and Devil meet in single combat". For here man pronounces his verdict upon the whole world, in the sense that he decides either for Being—that is to say, for being in God; or for nothingness—that is to say, for flight from God into Not-being. The whole tragedy played out on the two lower levels provides only the materials for the construction, and the symbols for the interpretation, of the sovereign tragedy of the God-like spiritual being's final self-determination: an act which is solely that of the free will.

To the external life, with all its spiritual oscillations, errors, masqueradings, illusions and self-deceptions Dostoevsky pays heed only in order to catch from it the phrase that decisively characterizes the personality: "Thy will be done", or, on the contrary, "My will be done, in spite of Thine". That is why the whole examination made by this celestial Inquisitor and metaphysical magistrate—his searching enquiry into all particulars—has a single aim: to ascertain the part played by the intelligible act of will in the empirical deed.

The results of this examination are radically different from sentences pronounced upon earthly culprits. In *The Brothers Karamazov*, for example, the chief culprit is not the murderer—a bastard and servant, who in envy and revengefulness repudiates his own goodwill towards a brother and master for whom he feels both hatred and a sense of affinity, with the result that he maliciously catches hold of the latter's scarcely uttered promptings and puts them into terrible effect. The chief culprit is the murderer's tempter, Ivan, whose meanly selfish personality decides neither for God nor against Him, but allows free play to the Powers of Darkness; thus basely betraying God's cause by a sort of metaphysical *abulia*.

But this is Ivan's secret, known only to himself and to God: the external retribution, pronounced by God, is brought upon the other brother, Dimitri, by a mistaken verdict of the jury—who are anxious to get rid of him and are eager to "do in" the alleged parricide.

Dimitri had, in fact, desired the death of his father. But how is this transitory emotion related to the categories of the intelligible will? Does not this tortured soul sing its "Amen" to the Creator of the universe? Yet a part of his Ego paralyses, by its chaotic resistance, the original will of the Ego as a whole: that will to God which is at the same time God's will, the will of the Son to the Father and the will of the Father to the Son.

This passionate element in Dimitri's nature had to seek its purification in suffering; because everything must suffer that breaks away from the primary source of Being. Thus human blindness becomes the instrument of Divine Providence, and the curse becomes a boon.

Here we touch the essence of tragedy: that which gives its own stamp to all literature that analyses and epitomizes life as Dostoevsky does. True tragedy, like true mysticism, is possible only on the soil of a deeply realistic view of the world. The tragic struggle must be fought out between the actual and the effective realities. Amongst these realities Dostoevsky, the "realist in the higher sense" ("in the mystical sense"—is what he should have said) includes, apart from the absolute reality of God, also many worlds of *noumenal* entities, to whom plainly belong human personalities. The tragedy is enacted between God and the human soul, it is mirrored in the latter's incarnation, and made manifold in the relations of man to man.

Be it from the original hatred of God; be it from the arrogance and blindness of the human sophistry that has turned away from God; or be it, lastly, from the darkness of a soul possessed by raging passions: whatever the cause, again and again flares up the tragedy of life, in the form of a struggle between the divine principle in the Creature and the power of "the Prince of this World";

the tragedy wherein "the good man in his dark eon-straint" either enters, like Dimitri Karamazov, upon a heart-rending conflict with his own higher and better self, or else, like Prince Myshkin the "Idiot"—who sees the world as perfect harmony and peace in God, but longs for complete embodiment and active participation in life and suffering, without being able to understand and to undergo the law of human life—the "Idiot" who becomes the victim of life.

6

Finally, if we turn to Dostoevsky's attitude towards Nature and feeling for Nature, we discover many a characteristic trait that helps us to understand his mystical realism. With truly paradoxical timidity, he avoids that common practice, which writers find so tempting, of adorning tales of human action with descriptions of scenery. It is as though he had taken an oath never to become what the lyrical poet Fet calls "an idle spectator of Nature". He seems to think it unseemly to offer an arbitrary, subjective interpretation—"in human, all-too-human style"—of Nature's secret life; to seek to mirror oneself in her, or to mirror Nature in man's spirit, which has severed itself from her.

Dostoevsky feels the need to kiss the earth in reverence, to nestle against it in childlike meekness. But extremely seldom does he permit himself to speak of Nature; and then only at significant and solemn moments, to call attention to her eternal and immutable symbolism. Thus in the epilogue to *Crime and Punishment* he cursorily describes the boundless steppe of the nomads, in order to contrast the wanderings of a personality that pursues empty visions, in futile and self-destructive madness,

41

with calm, impersonal Asia, the cradle of the human race, where still today graze the herds of Abraham. Thus, too, at a significant and sacred moment in the life of Alyosha, he causes us to gaze with Alyosha at a starry sky. Thus, again, a little star shines over a dark alley in St. Petersburg, whilst down below wanders a helpless, hunted girl, like a star fallen from the sky. Thus, in the same *Dream of a Queer Fellow*, "the tender emerald-green sea washes the shore in open, obvious, almost conscious love". Thus, in *The Possessed*, a park on an autumn night rears itself chaotically over the murdered Shatov.

Yet Dostoevsky is in no way a depicter of outward forms and faces. He seeks to catch men's inner likenesses; and in Nature, too, he wishes to see only its soul. But Nature has no changeably fluctuating psyche like that of man, and only human fancifulness can see in her any human characteristics. Her soul is not the modality of superficial events, but the substantiality of mystic depths. In the utterances of Father Zosima the curtain concealing this secret life is sometimes lifted; and a poor simpleton, Maria Timofeyevna in *The Possessed*, reveals to us, in a child's language and in the symbols of her childlike clairvoyance, ineffable truths:

" 'But I believe,' says I, 'that God and Nature are all the same thing'. And they all shouted out with one voice: 'You don't say !' The abbess laughed, and began whispering with the lady. She called me to her and patted me, and the lady gave me a pink scarf—would you like me to show it to you? Yes, and the little monk at once began teaching me, and everything he said was so friendly and so gentle and, it seems, so full of understanding. I sit there and listen. 'Do you understand?' says he. 'No,' says I, 'I haven't understood anything, and I'd rather you all left me quite in peace,' says I.

And since then they really have left me quite in peace. And about this time an old woman, who was doing penance in our midst for her soothsayings, whispers to me leaving the church: 'What is the Mother of God, do you think?' And says I, 'She's the Great Mother, the firm hope of the human race.' 'That's right,' says she. 'The Mother of God is the great Mother Earth, and she offers great joy to men. And every sorrow of the Earth, and every tear she sheds, is a joy to us. Let your tears water the Earth at your feet but half an ell deep, and in that same hour all will make for joy. And never again will you have any worry—any worry at all. That's the prophecy,' says she. And I've kept her words in my heart. And now, whenever I bow deeply in prayer I always kiss the Earth. I kiss it and weep. And I tell you, Shatushka, there's nothing wrong in these tears— and if you have no worry at all, the tears will come for sheer joy. The tears come of themselves, that's the way of it. Sometimes I go down to the shore of the lake. On the one side is our convent, on the other side is our peaky mountain—that's its name, Peaky Mountain. And so I go up this mountain and turn my face to the East, and fall on the ground and weep and weep—I don't know how long I go on weeping—and then I forget everything and no longer know what's happening. Then I get up and set off home, and the sun is setting—so big and mighty and beautiful—don't you love looking at the sun, Shatushka? It's a good thing to do, but sad, too. And I turn back towards the East, and the shadow, the shadow of our mountain, runs like an arrow straight across the lake—narrow and long, a whole verst long— out to the island in the lake, and splits this rocky island, just as it lies, into two halves; and, while it's splitting the island like this, the sun sets altogether, and everything is suddenly blotted out. Then suddenly all my longing seizes me, and memory comes back to me. I become afraid of the darkness, Shatushka, and weep still more for my little child."

Dostoevsky deliberately makes the obscure words of the simpleton sound alluring to the ears of religious people; whereas the true meaning of her utterances is far removed from the pantheism that these utterances appear to proclaim—a pantheism whose philosophic formulation sounds, from the simpleton's lips, like a naïve reminiscence of some learned phrase that she has somewhere read or heard, and, of course, misunderstood. Otherwise the writer could hardly have suggested that she feels at one with Nature, who, like her, dreams of the hotly awaited heavenly Bridegroom; that she is only the voice of Mother Earth, who, in her, is anxiously eager that this beautiful sun shall be only a promise of that unsetting sun, Jesus Christ, which will one day clothe her in its robe of light.

In her clairvoyance Maria Timofeyevna unconsciously beholds the Christian mystery in the eternal liturgy of Nature. The peaky mountain, whose shadow, as it cleaves the rocky island, makes the sign of the Cross, stands for Golgotha; and the sun stands for the Lamb of God. The little child for whom she weeps is only a fancy; yet, without this imaginary mourning for a child, the picture of this soul racked by the expectation of the distant Bridegroom, the beloved Redeemer, would be incomplete.

> A fine new house I do not crave,
>   This tiny cell suffices me;
> There will I dwell, my soul to save,
>   And ever pray to God for thee.[1]

---

[1] Translation from the Russian original by Constance Garnett.

The words of this little song are perhaps Dostoevsky's most tender expression of the innermost longing of the Creature, of the secret anchoretism of Mother Earth, who is the deeply expectant bride. According to the legend of the convent of Divej, near Sarov, the Mother of God arrived at the settlement and indicated the lodging that she would later occupy. So, too, according to the Homeric hymn, did the sorrowful Mother Demeter arrive, after her long wanderings, at Eleusis, and there retire into holy seclusion.

Dostoevsky's mystical realism, which has its roots in the ancient conception of a living Mother Earth, flourishes in the mythological interpretation of the universal life. The validity of the tragic principle, which governs the relations between God and humanity, is extended, beyond the human sphere, to all creation subordinate to man, and has correlates in the hidden inner life of Nature; who, conceived of as a living entity is dependent upon the final self-destination of man, and is, in her own fashion, aware of this dependence. Mother Earth, who ultimately represents all Nature, and to whom Dostoevsky offers a special worship, is drawn into the mystery of the Passion of the Son of Man. Man bears against her an ancient guilt, and increases it by his sinfulness; but also by his sanctification he achieves her redemption, which shall be granted to her at the end of time through man's glorification in Christ.

More will be said on this subject in the next section of this book, in which Dostoevsky is considered as a creator of myth.

Part II

Mythological Aspect

Part II

Mythological Aspect

Μυθολογούμενα

IN their inner structure Dostoevsky's novels are tragedies in epic dress; but, if their deepest content and artistic intention are examined, they seem to depict supra-personal, metaphysical events. These events, however, are such that neither can the artist describe them, nor can we witness them, otherwise than in the flood-tide of external action and personal psychology; by means of which they acquire reality in the life of man and of mankind.

Dostoevsky has a peculiarly characteristic conception of life as a drama·which, both in the fate of the individual and in the history of the world, is enacted invisibly— beneath the empirically recognizable pragmatism of events and the surface of spiritual impulses—by God and the innermost human Ego. And from this conception arises, of itself, that inherent symbolism of his epic-tragedy, that "realism in the higher sense", as he himself calls it (see page 37), which we shall term realistic symbolism.

Realistic symbolism in art leads the soul of the spectator *a realibus ad realiora*, which latter reveal themselves in *realibus*; from reality on the lower plane, a reality of lesser ontological value, to the more real reality. Meanwhile the artist's discovery and development of his

49

theme is moving in the opposite direction; inasmuch as the artist who aims at realistic symbolism descends from an intuitive comprehension of the higher reality to its incarnation in the lower reality—*a realioribus ad realia.*

If one wishes fully to understand the epic-tragedy, one must discover in its hidden depths a nucleus that is epic in form, but tragic in its presentation of inner antagonism; a nucleus that contains from the beginning the full symbolic force of the whole work, its entire "higher realism": that is to say, the original intuition of a transcendental reality, and of the event as taking place within this reality, which determines the epical fabric of action in the world of the senses. To describe this nucleus of symbolic creation we use the word "myth".

By "myth" we mean a synthetic proposition in which to the subject-symbol is attached a verbal predicate. In the oldest epoch of religions, this was the pattern of the primitive myth as a verbal expression of the fundamental idea, and as the determining factor of the form of rite associated with it. The rite seeks either to enhance by sympathetic magic the power of the action proclaimed in the verbal predicates, or to nullify it by counter-magic.

It is only later that out of the rite grows the luxuriant mass of myth, which is usually of an etiological nature— that is to say, seeking to offer an interpretation of the significance of the cult.

As examples of the primitive myth may be offered: "the sun—is born", "the sun—dies", "God—enters man", "Heaven—by means of rain, makes fruitful its spouse, Earth". Is there not a great similarity to these, even today, in the synthetic propositions that make up the true content of all poetic communication? For in the language of poetry all propositions are synthetic; and it is for this reason alone that they are so delightfully fresh and naïve, so unexpected and so full of a spontaneous inner life, whose discovery in the most familiar phenomena fills us with surprise. (" . . . a gentle wind blows from the azure sky, Still stands the myrtle and the bay-tree waves on high.") When the symbol—that is to say, any object of pure poetic contemplation—is enriched by the verbal predicate, it receives life and movement; and the unconscious symbolism that is peculiar to all true poetry becomes, in a sense, myth-forming.[1]

---

[1]"The original cult (which constant repetition, hallowed by tradition, transforms into a rite) implies and confirms by its direct action symbolism a definite idea, removed from the emotional sphere, which, as soon as it finds expression in words, can be described as fore-myth. In contrast to the later unfolded myth, the fore-myth is simple and short. Its pragmatical element is still undeveloped, and therefore cannot yet obscure its essential content. The primitive myth gives expression to—and exhausts—the original vision, in the form of a synthetic proposition in which the subject is the name of the Godhead, or of the concrete object in the material world that has been animistically endowed with life and is regarded as a 'Daimon'; and the predicate is the verb that expresses the action, or state, attributed to this daemonic being.

"It is precisely this verbal predicate—which treats the subject of the fore-myth as a personality performing some action or undergoing some tribulation, and thus brings the principle of movement into man's conception of his surrounding world of polymorphous living entities and of the souls of things—it is this verbal predicate that creates the nucleus of later mythical narration.

"In so far as it is synthetic, the proposition contained in the fore-myth, as it becomes perceptible, awakes a feeling of astonishment, by means of the unexpectedness of the connection revealed between the subject and the action, and either provokes primeval man to reflection or conveys to him an impression of something mysterious and incomprehensible.

"It is more appropriate to speak of the fore-myth as being 'experienced' or 'made real' than as being 'presented' in the rite. For the rite has existed longer than intellectual conceptions; it endures, whereas the energy necessary for the lively re-creation of the fore-myth in the consciousness gradually fails, and its original brightness and noble simplicity continually fade and waste away.

"At this point the general attitude towards the rite becomes simultaneously shy and inquisitive; whilst the rite itself grows ever more obscure, and, as a result of outside influences—such as a tendency to syncretism and assimilation, an accumulation of magical elements, and the creation of new invocatory epithets and names for the Godhead—develops an ever-increasing complexity.

"In reply to the question, whence came the rite, or why does it have such-and-such features, arises the etiological fable, whose purpose is to confirm both the traditional character of the rite and also its authenticity. With undeviating adherence to the poetic and symbolic development of the fore-myth, the fable repeats the rite in the ideal projection of the myth, or in the ideally-historical projection of the legend. This is the only reason why it is possible to speak of a logic of the fore-myth, and of the absence of any arbitrariness in the creation of myths."—*From the author's "Dionysus and Fore-Dionysism."*

Truly realistic symbolism, based on the intuition of a higher reality, acquires a principle of life and movement (the verb of the myth) within the intuition itself as a comprehension of the dynamic principle of intelligible substance: as a discernment of its actual form, or, what is the same thing, a discernment of its universal actuality and its activity in the world.

The more the writer has the feeling for *realiora in realibus*—that pathos which breaks out in Goethe's "All that is transient is but an allegory"—the more naturally, of course, does he meet and conform with the original imaginative patterns of the essential train of thought that lives on in the obscure memory of the ancient myth.[1] Conversely, the more deeply the poetic conception is rooted in the native soil of the myth, the more significant and intrinsically true does it seem to us—that is, if we have not yet lost the sense of its magnetic force, so that Goethe's words "truth was discovered long ago" can still be fully applied to poetic truth.

---

[1] Ancient myth has survived into the present—preserved in the "wandering motive" and the "wandering theme" (as, for example, the saga of Orestes converted into the tragedy of Hamlet). We glimpse fragments of it where we would least expect them. (*Cf.* the motive of the crimson carpet in Emile Zola's *L'Argent*, which Wilamowitz, in his *Heracles*, recognizes as a reminiscence of Aeschylus's *Agamemnon*.) Even today ancient myth influences entire works of literature. (This is frequently true of Ibsen's works.)

Chapter I

THE ENCHANTED BRIDE

I

MYTH, in the sense explained above, must be what Dostoevsky himself refers to, in a letter concerning the work he was doing on *The Possessed*, when he speaks of the "artistic" idea that is arrived at in "poetic inspiration", and of the difficulty of capturing it by poetic composition.[1] The fact that this idea is basically the perception of a transcendental actuality hidden beneath the surge of external events, to which this actuality alone can give a meaning, is made plain by his comments on his alleged "idealism", which for him is, on the contrary, "realism in the higher sense".

"I have quite a different notion of reality and realism from that of our 'realist' literary critics. . . . My idealism is more real than their realism. If someone were merely to tell the story of the spiritual development through which we Russians have passed during the last ten years, wouldn't the realists raise an outcry that it was all sheer fantasy? Yet it would be genuine, pure realism. That sort of thing is, in fact, realism itself—only deeper than their realism, which floats very much on the surface. . . . Their realism cannot explain a hundredth part of all the real

---

[1]A letter to the philosopher Strakhov, dated April 23, 1871.

things that have happened. But our sort of realism has actually foretold some of these things."[1]

The only person who can grasp the inner meaning of all that happens is he who can see, behind the sequence of happenings, the hidden course of other, truly real events. But, to do this, one must have a special insight—an insight into the nature of supra-individual integers of will, and their relation to the individual will.

It is true that, when we contemplate the inner and real drama of history, we find that its characters are people; but they are not simply individual, self-determining personalities, but primarily vehicles of a corporate will, which realizes itself in their actions, and helps to determine these, whilst also being determined by them. On the historical plane, these people are both individuals *per se* and also instruments of a collective soul; even when they are only dimly, or not at all, aware of their very actual attachment to the supra-personal—and yet, in its own way, personal—Whole, within whose sphere of influence they reside.

How, then, does this attachment come about, and how may one conceive of the subject, and of the constitution of the corporate will?

For Dostoevsky, the personality has a natural antinomy. On the one hand, it is essentially integral: however numerous its fissures and contradictions—however lacerating its inward conflict—it must, in the end, unequivocally take its own decisions and fulfil its own destiny. On the other hand, and despite all this, it is not a self-contained entity. Indeed, its very integrality

[1]Letter to Maikov, dated December 11, 1868. The final words obviously allude to a remarkable corroboration of Dostoevsky's account of crime and the criminal (as given in *Crime and Punishment*), which appeared in a report published by the "Legal Chronicle" in 1866, the very year in which Dostoevsky's book was published. The report resembled Dostoevsky's story even in a number of apparently accidental details.

rests finally on the fact that, in a strange and peculiar manner, a higher integer comes to life within it: and it is precisely from its oneness with this integer that the personality draws the necessary strength for its separate existence.

Hallowed is the bond that binds the personality to its Whole, and thus makes it a part of true Being; for it is the characteristic of true Being that it reveals itself as unity in a diversity of aspects. Unhallowed, contrariwise, is the rash attempt of the individual wilfully to tear itself away from its Whole, which is rooted in the laws of Being; and such an attempt takes revenge upon itself, in the form of a daemonic isolation.

The personality, therefore, is separate from all other personalities, and yet at the same time bound in oneness with them. Its limits are indefinable and mysterious.

> Try to divide yourself; to determine where your personality ends and another personality begins. Try and do it by means of science! Science will surely take on the job! After all, Socialism bases itself on science. For Christianity, on the other hand, such a suggestion cannot even be put into words. What are the chances of this decision or of that? A new, an unexpected spirit will breathe.—*From Dostoevsky's Journal of an Author.*

Dostoevsky clearly recognizes that to the Christian spirit our negative definition of personality (I and not-I, Mine and not-Mine) is inacceptable. He demands that it should be turned into the positive. This is not a question of a spiritual 'transcension converting the negative self-experience into a positive one: it is a question of ontological first premises.

According to an argument contained in "Zosima's Literary Remains" (*The Brothers Karamazov*), mankind has not yet come to the end of the "period of solitude"; and it is just in our time that the danger of isolation, which is a kind of suicide, is most plainly showing itself. As soon, however, as the end of this period has been reached, suddenly everyone will realize the "unnaturalness" of isolation, and will begin to abhor it. Everyone will be amazed that we could have lived so long in darkness, not even guessing at the existence of light; and "then in Heaven will appear the sign of the Son of Man"—that is to say, the mystery of Christ will be made clear in the eyes of all men.[1]

Here dawns upon Dostoevsky the ineffable knowledge that each individual man is the whole of mankind, and that all mankind is the *one* man, the *one* Adam.

If personality is conceivable only in connection with that which has being; if it is the merging into a higher personal unity that forms the ontological basis of individual existence (that which sets saving limits to individuation), then it seems natural to assume that between the two bordering spheres—universal humanity and the human individual—there is a series of personal and syncretic unities, bearing the same relation to the Whole as the seven "Churches", "Candlesticks" or "Angels" in the *Revelation* of St. John the Divine bear to the one Church of God.

On the other hand, the force that struggles against the Divine All-Oneness, the force that drives the individual to the spiritual suicide of isolation, must always seek to evoke rebellious complexes of the soul—after the ancient example of the builders of the Tower of Babel—complexes which are, however, no true entities, and are

---

[1]Dostoevsky's influence can be clearly detected in the celebrated lectures of his young friend Vladimir Solovyev, given in 1881, on the humanity of God and the divinity of mankind—on the historical development of the human race, as a distinct unit, into the mystical body of Christ.

to be ranged with that daemonic "Legion" of which we shall speak later.

2

It is therefore not surprising that Dostoevsky conceives of the people as a personality—and not as a personality synthesized by thought, but as independent in essence and as an integral being. It has a peripheral diversity of aspects, and also an inner holiness, that of the one and integral awareness, of the one and integral will.

We must have recourse to the Bible to obtain a clear picture of this. The concept of peoples as personalities and as angels underlies the whole historical philosophy and eschatology of the Scriptures.[1]

In the metaphysical unity of the people two principles may be distinguished. One is feminine and pertaining to the soul; the other is masculine and pertaining to the spirit. The first has its roots in the universal Mother, the living Earth, as a mystical entity; the second corresponds, in the personality of the people, to something like the Platonic ἡγεμονικόν, and may be termed, in Apocalyptic language, the Angel of the people. The free self-determination of the conscious character, the decision to be either for God or against Him—which, as already said, forms the nucleus of the personal tragedy of the human individual—is the proper function of this spirit; which, within its own sphere of power, is the people's guide. This spirit decides for the whole people, and thereby determines its historical fate.

---

[1] In propounding his theory of the nation, Dostoevsky seeks the support of the authority of the Church: this becomes especially clear in his later work. But he does not draw a sharp enough distinction between the concepts of Nation and of Church; with the result that, despite all his efforts to remain faithful to the "oecumenical" principle, he falls into the error of ecclesiastical nationalism.

It must not be forgotten, however, that this decision is taken as an act inherent in the will of the people itself. The spirit of the people can rest upon its own self, it can lock its doors against the Divine Logos; or, on the other hand, it can renounce its selfish Ego and, through the human beings that it has chosen for the task, bring to Earth the tidings that it bears God within itself. Only by bearing God within itself can the people's Ego become universal, the Ego of the whole of mankind.

Lastly, historical evolution can occasion still a third contingency: a kind of estrangement of the Angel from the people, a temporary indecision or impotence of the masculine principle. This is, inevitably, exploited by the Powers of Evil, who thereupon attempt to form a "Legionary" group-soul of human beings inimical to God; and, by means of this, to snatch unto themselves the office of spiritual leadership; to dominate the people's soul and throw it into a blind frenzy.

Dostoevsky believes that the Russian people is a "God-bearing" people. The God-bearing people is, by definition, not the empirical people, although the empirical people constitutes the former's terrestrial body. The God-bearing people is, in its essence, neither an ethnographical nor even a political concept. It is one of the flames of the many-branched candlestick of the mystical Church: a candlestick that sheds its light before the Throne of the Word. Nation and State receive consecration and meaning only in so far as they are vessels of the God-bearing spirit. The outer shell of this spirit may appear sinful; it may be, in fact, sinful, maimed and decaying: but the spirit bloweth where it listeth. The God-bearing people is a living light that shines in the Church, and it is also an Angel of the Lord: yet, until the world comes to an end, the Angel is free in his choice of ways; and, if his loyalty wavers, there comes down upon him the threat of the Apocalypse: "I will remove thy candlestick out of his place, except thou repent."

It is therefore impossible to *know* anything about Russia with entire certainty. "One can only *believe* in Russia", as was said by Tyutchev, whose ideas on this subject closely resembled Dostoevsky's. Dostoevsky, too, simply *believed* in Russia. This is why, in the spirit of Christian hope, he greeted the coming salvation, which he envisaged as the Kingdom of Christ on Russian soil, with his cry of "so be it, so be it!"[1]

Dostoevsky, who approaches the idea of God-bearing all-oneness in *Crime and Punishment*, and the idea of the eternally-feminine principle in *The Idiot* (as he did previously in *The Landlady*), also arrived, through meditation on Russia's possession by the daemons of godlessness and self-will, at a positive perception of the mysterious connections between these two entities. When these perceptions flamed into full brightness, his novel *The Possessed*—which had previously seemed unhappily conceived and likely to be still-born—suddenly shone before him in a dazzling new light. In his "creative excitement", Dostoevsky set about the rebuilding of the structure upon which he had already started; seeking, and at the same time doubting, whether he could give expression and shape to the whole mighty greatness of the "idea" that he had come to behold.

He had seen with his own eyes, so to speak, how the masculine principle of the people's innermost being—the principle directed towards the ideal of contemplative spirituality—can allow its influence upon the psyche of

---

[1]*Cf.* the author's *Die Russische Idee* (Tübingen-Mohr, 1930), pp. 15, 20.

the people, and upon the external life as a whole, to be supplanted by daemonic "Legion". He had seen, too, how the feminine principle, which is the soul of the Earth of Russia, is filled with torment and with longing for her deliverer, the hero in Christ, the God-bearer. Though, in her bondage and forsakenness, her behaviour may be chaotic, she will always recognize the traitor and usurper who approaches her wearing the mask of Him whom she yearns for and yearningly awaits. She will recognize him, expose him and curse him.

The Myth was born.

3

In *The Possessed* Dostoevsky tried to show how the eternally-feminine principle in the Russian soul has to suffer violence and oppression at the hands of those Daemons who in the people contend against Christ for the mastery of the masculine principle in the people's consciousness.[1] He sought to show how these Daemons, in their attack upon the Russian soul, also wound the Mother of God herself (as shown in the symbolic episode of the desecration of the ikon), although their vilifications cannot reach her invisible depths (compare the symbol of the untouched silver garment of the Virgin Undefiled in the home of the murdered Maria Timofeyevna). Since the basic theme of the novel is the symbolism of the relationship between the Earth's soul, the daring, erring human spirit and the Powers of Evil, it was quite natural that Dostoevsky should be confronted by a presentation of this myth which had already been attempted in the world's literature—although with a different orientation,

---

[1]"Whence come the Nihilists? They come from nowhere, for they have always been with us, in us, and around us."—*From Dostoevsky's Notes.*

and without any allusion to the idea of the mission of the Redeemer: namely, in Goethe's *Faust*[1]

Maria Timofeyevna took the place of Gretchen; who, after the disclosures in the second part of the tragedy, is identified, as a manifestation of the eternally-feminine, both with Helen and with Mother Earth. Nicolai Stavrogin is the Russian Faust: but in a negative version, since love has been quenched in him, and, with it, the indefatigable striving—erotic, in the Platonic sense—through which Faust is saved.

The rôle of Mephisto is assumed by Peter Verhovensky, who at decisive moments emerges from behind Stavrogin, faithfully imitating the grimaces of his prototype. The relation between Gretchen and the Mater Gloriosa is the same as that between Maria Timofeyevna and the Mother of God. Maria's terror at Stavrogin's appearance in her room is prefigured in Margarete's scene of madness in the prison. Maria's imaginary mourning for a child is almost the same emotion as that which finds expression in Gretchen's hallucinated memories. Maria's song (*cf.* page 44) is the song of the Russian soul, a mysterious symbol of the deep life in its inward "cell".

Maria pays for the beloved that he may remain true, not so much to herself, but rather to his destiny as a God-bearer; and she patiently awaits him, fearful and doing penance to earn his deliverance. Similarly, Gretchen turns, in her song, from the old King of the farthest West, of *Ultima Thule*, and from his sun-goblet, to the distant beloved, and touchingly adjures the latter to keep faith—by returning as a new sun.

She who sings the song of love in her inward cell is not only a "medium" of Mother Earth (the late Hellenic

---

[1] Goethe's influence on Dostoevsky can be detected even in the latter's early work, *The Insulted and Injured*. In creating Nelly, Dostoevsky may have had in mind the image of Mignon.

scholars who classified ecstasies and trances would have called her "one possessed by Earth"—κατόχος ἐκ τῆς Γῆς), but also Mother Earth's symbol. In the myth she represents the soul of earth, under the specific aspect of Russian earth. That is why she has her little mirror in her hand: the universal soul is perpetually reflected in Nature. Moreover, it is not accidental that she is the wedded wife of the protagonist of the tragedy, Nicolai Stavrogin. Nor is it accidental that she is not truly his wife, but retains her virginity.

"The Prince of this World" has dominion over the world's soul, but is unable to achieve a real power over it. In just the same way the Samaritan woman of the Fourth Book of the Gospels is not the wife of him whom she took as her sixth husband.

As though gifted with clairvoyance, Maria Timofeyevna, when she has recovered from her first fright, obstinately addresses Stavrogin as "Prince", opposing him in the same time to another true *him*.

> "I must have done *him* some wrong, some very great wrong—only I don't know what it is: that's what will plague me for ever. . . . I pray and pray, and always I think of the great wrong I have done *him*."[1]

This other Prince, the Prince of Light, is the God-bearing hero in whose person Maria, clairvoyante in her Christian simplicity, expects to behold the Prince of Glory.

Even Maria's lameness is a sign of her secret guilt of hostility to God[2]: the guilt of a half-heartedness and disloyalty that perhaps were present in her from the beginning; or, at least, of imperfect loyalty, of a pri-

---

[1] Translation from the Russian original by Constance Garnett.
[2] Concerning lameness as the mystical sign of the fight with God, see *Genesis* xxxii, 24-32.

mordial resistance to the bridegroom who deserted her, as Eros deserts Psyche—who, because of an original sin inherent in her mortal being, is sinful in the sight of the Divine love.

> "What—aren't you a Prince? I was ready to expect anything from *his* enemies, but such insolence, never! Is he still alive? Have you killed him, or haven't you? Confess. ... Tell me, you impostor, did you get a lot for it? Did you ask a big price? A curse upon you. ..."

The "blind owl", the "wretched actor", "Grishka Otrepiev, burdened with the curse of seven Ecclesiastical Councils"[1], "Judas Iscariot", the "Devil" himself, he who has supplanted (and perhaps also destroyed, or, at least, somehow betrayed) the "noble falcon" that "lives somewhere behind the mountains, and soars to gaze at the sun": such are the elements of the "evil dream" that Maria Timofeyevna dreams before the coming of Stavrogin; a dream that returns to her, in her prophetic delirium, when she is in fact awake. With the same clairvoyance Gretchen directly recognizes the nature and aura of Mephisto, which make her loathe the person of her beloved.

4

But who is Nicolai Stavrogin? Dostoevsky provides a clear token of his great significance: it is not by chance that his name is derived from the Greek word for the Cross ($\sigma\tau\alpha\nu\rho\acute{o}s$). Secret signs foretell for him a sort of royal anointment. In the eyes of beholders he is the legendary prince, Ivan the Tsarevitch: all who come near him feel the strange, superhuman fascination that he exercises. Upon him is shed the grace of a mystical

---

[1] The "false Demetrius", synonym of an impostor.

comprehension of the ultimate secrets of the people's soul and its expectation of the God-bearer. He initiates Shatov and Kirillov into the prime mysteries of Russian Messianism. He implants in their souls a deep sense of Christ—together with the most deep doubt of God's existence.

He himself, however, at some decisive moment of his half-hidden and terrible past, has betrayed the holiness that offered itself to him. After his loss of faith in God he gives himself up to practical Satanism, and holds with Satan hallucinated conversations. Accepting no reward, he is not Satan's debtor—as Faust was—but his vassal. He gives Satan his life, which had been promised to Christ, and is thereby condemned to carry a void within himself until, whilst still in his earthly life, he is over-taken by the "other death"; which "other death" manifests itself as an annihilation of the personality within the living body. Spiritually he has died long ago, and all that now remains of him is his fascinatingly beautiful mask.

But the Powers of Evil need him, need his mask—they need him as a vessel of their own will and an executant of their practical purpose: he has already lost his own will. A traitor in the sight of Christ, he is also disloyal to Satan. He must put himself, as a mask, at Satan's disposal, so that this false visage may mislead the world; so that he may play the part of a false Tsarevitch, who will let loose the revolt of the masses: and he finds within himself no will towards this. He becomes unfaithful to the Revolution, and to Russia herself. (Symbols of this: his assumption of a foreign nationality, and especially his wilful abandonment of his wife Maria Timofeyevna.) He becomes unfaithful to everything and everyone, and hangs himself like Judas before he has reached the diabolic cave that he has hollowed out for himself in a dark, precipitous ravine. But his betrayal of Satan does not exempt him from his passive rôle of susceptible intermediary and vehicle for the devilish "Legion" (*St. Mark* v, 9), which gains dominion, around him and by his agency, over the herd of the possessed.[1] They are a herd, and no more, for each of them has in some sort been deprived of his Ego: in each the living Ego is paralysed, and into its place an alien will has entered.

Only two of the people with whom Stavrogin comes into contact have not surrendered their Ego, and are thus separate from the herd: Kirillov and Shatov. How did these two retain command over their Ego? Did these most gifted of Stavrogin's disciples invent for themselves an imaginary homunculus, as Faust's disciple succeeded in doing?

5

Kirillov, who at nights drinks tea by himself and broods over his own destiny in almost solipsistic self-absorption, asserts his autonomous freedom by a sort of flight from the world. He is, in Nietzsche's phrase, a true "hermit of the spirit", and what he asserts is not so much his outer independence—though he guards this jealously—as his imaginary metaphysical self-sufficiency, which is what makes him fundamentally an enemy of God. Nevertheless, he keeps a gentle light burning before the image of Christ, which in some fashion of his own he knows and loves.

---

[1] The passage from *St. Mark* where mention is made of devils—which, after the healing of the man possessed by Legion, entered into a herd of swine—is used as a preliminary epigraph to Dostoevsky's book. Concerning the symbolism of Legion, *cf.* below Part III (Daemonology), end of Section 5.

Since he holds that there is no preter-human reality corresponding to man's conception of God, he considers it logically necessary that man himself should become God: Jesus, he thinks, would have become God even if He had not believed in the Heavenly Father. But man can become God only after he has conquered that "anguish of the fear of death" which he previously called God. To proclaim and seal this conquest, man must perform an act of absolute disobedience. This act can take the form only of suicide—a suicide not caused by misery and affliction, but committed in untrammelled wilfulness and in full acceptance of life. Man must himself mount the empty throne of God, which has been built by man's fear of death.

Such are the views of this atheist-mystic, whose mania anticipates that of Nietzsche, the modern Ixion. Christ alone did not fear death: so Kirillov also will not fear it. Moreover, he must climb the Golgotha of a freely chosen self-pride—he must kill himself, for his own sake. . . .

Thus, in the blindness of arrogance and the wilderness of his spirit, Kirillov sets out to achieve his anti-Christian sacrifice: his anti-Golgotha; a "Man-become-God", as a negative version of God-become-Man; a being that sought to preserve its personality and therefore destroyed itself—that recognized its ˌSonship, but sought to establish this upon a denial of the Father.

In the terrible end of this dreamer smitten with God-sickness, Dostoevsky wished to show that atheism, in a personality awakened to ontological self-awareness, ends in metaphysical madness. If a man of higher nature persuades himself, as Kirillov did, that "he must believe that he does not believe in God" (Dostoevsky may at this point have had in mind Bakunin's formulation, which was being much discussed at this time, of the

incompatibility between faith in God and human freedom), then he feels himself irresistibly driven to
self-deification and self-destruction.

Kirillov is by no means an egoistical character. He is
noble, compassionate, ready to help others. He has a
tender sympathy and love for all living creatures, and
with Heraclitean enthusiasm he extols life in all its beauty
and self-contradiction. Nay, more, he knows moments
of ineffable bliss in the ecstatic contemplation of the
harmony of the universe. It is only the fear of death—
"the old God"—that, in his view, spoils human existence
and turns men into slaves. That is why he vows to
perform the act of redemption—the slaying of the old
God through his own suicide; and it is also the reason
why he divides history into two epochs: the first lasting
from the ape to the slaying of God, and the second from
the slaying of God to the completely, "even physically",
proclaimed transmutation of man into "Man-become-
God". Thus, he believes, must the insidious symbol of
"God-become-Man" be recast.

This sombre fanatic certainly does not belong to
the "herd" of the possessed; nor has it any need of
him (it needs leaders of quite another stamp: a Peter
Verhovensky, perhaps; or a Shigalov, who, in order to
ensure a public welfare based on the principle of equality,
seeks to exterminate every germ of higher spirituality,
and decrees that all individual heads that in any way rise
above the throng must be cut off). Nevertheless, in
Dostoevsky's view Kirillov is one of the possessed,
since he is diseased with the primitive hatred of God:
which Dostoevsky regards as the strongest motive force
of the daemonic assault.

6

Shatov, too, never surrendered his Ego to "Legion". Indeed, he rebelled against the Daemons, and for this was torn in pieces by them. Nevertheless, he, too, is a carrier of the virus. At best he is only a convalescent. When asked whether, amidst all his talk of the God-bearing people, he really believes in God, he stammers in embarrassment: "I want to—I shall believe." He wishes to merge his Ego in the people's Ego, yet at the same time to establish that the people's Ego is the Ego of Christ. He shrank from the Daemons, but began to waver in his belief in the people.[1] The falsehood of his attitude towards Christ is shown in the fact that he could not, through Christ, behold the Father. He drew bright revelations from the poisoned well of Stavrogin's soul, and, like his mystagogic master, misapplied them: arriving at the conclusion that the Russian Christ was the people itself, whose mission was to incarnate its spiritual and masculine principle in its coming Messiah, in order through this Messiah (thus, again, through an impostor) to proclaim: "I am the Bridegroom."

It is a mistake to accuse Shatov the mystic of making the Godhead an attribute of the people. On the contrary, he seeks, as he himself says, to elevate the people to Godhead. The blow in the face that he deals Stavrogin is an inevitable act: the heretic punishes the heresiarch for his treachery. Stavrogin refused to become the Russian "Christ", and thus betrayed Shatov's faith and shattered his life.

Nevertheless, this waverer has at least the merit of having wavered away from the herd, and of having, when all is said, found faith in the Earth's soul. This is

---

[1] The name Shatov is derived from "shatkij"—"wavering".

why Maria Timofeyevna, in her simplicity, feels him to be her friend. Thanks to his love of the true Christ—a love which, false and dim though it be, is rooted in the primitive element of his oneness with the people— "Shatushka" is illumined by the reflected glow of a Grace that has been shed upon him. He appears as a magnanimous, all-forgiving champion and guardian of the feminine soul in its sin and humiliation (as is especially shown in his behaviour towards his wife), and dies a martyr.

From an early age—probably ever since his years of imprisonment—Dostoevsky had pondered over the spiritual mission of the Russian people. Later he speaks of "the independent Russian idea", which his homeland must "bring forth with fearful pangs", and even refers to its "labour-pains" as having already begun.

The riddle propounded in that prophetically inspired work, *The Possessed*, is connected with the nexus of problems contained in this expectation. What is the spiritual meaning of the secret yearning of the Russian Earth for Redemption and the Redeemer? How will the coming of the hero in Christ, her Ivan the Tsarevich —heralded in her prophetic dreams of her God-bearing mission—how will this coming manifest itself? In other words, how can the land of "wise will and wild action", which for ages has been entitled "holy", become indeed "Holy Russia", and the people become the Church? How does a thing, impossible for man, become possible for God?

Dostoevsky begins to dream of the mysterious Messenger of the inspired Father Zosima, as being one of "the pure and elect", founders of a new race and a new life" already heralded in *Crime and Punishment*.

Chapter II

THE REVOLT AGAINST MOTHER EARTH

I

THE theme of Psyche oppressed by the Powers of Evil and awaiting her deliverer had exercised Dostoevsky's mind even before he started work on *The Possessed*. For him it was by no means merely a literary theme: after all, St. Paul (*Epistle to the Romans* viii, 19-23) wrote that the Creature groans in pain as it waits for its deliverance by the sons of God. For Dostoevsky, the problem thus indicated had a direct and close connection with the destinies of Russia. It was in the hope of clearing a path to its solution by the agency of art that he sketched the outline of *The Idiot*; but, during the execution of this mighty project, other relationships and basic materials came to the fore. What chiefly prevented him, however, from being satisfied with the project was simply the fact that the answer given in *The Idiot* to the question concerning the possibility of a God-bearing hero proved in the end to be negative.

It was not until he wrote *The Brothers Karamazov* that Dostoevsky found the answer he sought, in the mission of a Russian lay brother who at the bidding of his spiritual superiors leaves his monastery and goes out into the world; and in Alyosha's obedience to the call and his enactment of its purpose.

But this work, so rich in significance, is incomplete, and the author's last, solemn word remains unspoken. It is significant, however, that Alyosha's lame fiancée is cured by the Grace-giving virtue of his proximity, and secretly also by the miracle performed by his master, Zosima; whereas the lame woman in *The Possessed* perishes miserably. Psyche has at last found her deliverer.

Yet this work, which was undertaken only after a religious preparation, is in conception allegorical and didactic rather than mythological. Thus, "historical allegories" is an apt description of the main themes of the plot: the irreconcilable conflict between the father, who seems to represent the erstwhile ruling class (which is now overthrown and morally degenerate), and his elder sons; the parricide committed by the social outcast amongst the brothers, but inspired and secretly arranged by the learned son, the theoretical pioneer of revolution; the supposed guilt, and actual expiation, imposed upon the eldest brother, who incarnates the spirit of the nation, in all its brighter and darker aspects; and lastly the act of healing (beginning only after the forcible expulsion of the old evil, and at first scarcely perceptible) performed by the elect among the younger generation. On the other hand, this last work of Dostoevsky presents directly religious truth, and shows the effect, bordering on the miraculous, that it has upon life. Its pure white light, tempered to our vision by thin veils, shines directly in our eyes, not refracted in the coloured intermediate plane of myth and imagination.

This change of artistic approach essentially distinguishes the master's last creative period from the period that gave birth to *The Possessed* and *The Idiot* for the period of these earlier works, on the contrary, was dominated by the mythical element, which we are here primarily discussing.

Having recognized the "artistic idea" (Dostoevsky's phrase) of *The Possessed* as a contribution to the corpus of myth, we shall now attempt a similar investigation of *The Idiot*. To start with, however, we shall study the fundamental creative activity that constituted the preliminary approach to the thought-content of this work. Dostoevsky's meditations on the hero of *Crime and Punishment* had already provided him with his aim: to show the true greatness of one who is meek, of a man of "goodwill" in the Christian sense; and thus, by proving the possibility of such a positive character, and his actual effectiveness upon present-day life, to call out, as it were, to his contemporaries: "We bid you hope!"

The apostate from humanity as One being made of soul and spirit—he who renounces humanity, and consequently Mother Earth—such a one "splits off"[1] and thus himself becomes split: the intellectual and criminal Raskolnikov, who is saved by the self-sacrifice of a meek feminine soul; or, on the other hand, the martyr to the faith in humanity as a spiritual integer, the holy "Idiot" Myshkin, who loves the Earth more than his primitive memory of the other-worldly home, and has come to rescue the feminine soul from bondage and desecration—for Dostoevsky these two are the poles of a *single* conception. The Luciferian self-assertion of the personality that strives meanly to preserve itself, and greedily to increase its wealth, is opposed to the generous self-surrender of the soul that, following the precept of the New Testament, does not fear to lose itself.

---

[1] In Russian, Raskolnikov comes from the word "Raskol", that means "split", "schism", "heresy"; "Raskolnik" "apostate", "heretic".

The opposition is shown between alienation from Earth[1] and oneness with it; between defection from men and union with them; between efforts to rise from poverty and weakness to power and fame, and the renunciation and impoverishment ($\kappa\acute{\epsilon}\nu\omega\sigma\iota\varsigma$) of an over-abundant spiritual force born in the light of grace; between the slow climb towards the light, and the sudden plunge into darkness—like that of a shooting star.

All these contrasts illustrate also the respective motives of the myths of those two antithetical works, *The Idiot* and *Crime and Punishment*. Before studying the former, let us contemplate the underlying mythical conceptions of the latter.

2

The action of *Crime and Punishment* takes place in St. Petersburg. Dostoevsky could discover no more suitable location and background for the tragedy of the illusive presumption and rebellion of One against All, of the individual against Heaven and Earth. Nowhere else, in his opinion, did the *genius loci* produce so dreadful a fever of the soul, such fantastic, and at the same time abstract, visions and ventures of delirium.

Is not St. Petersburg itself—that magnificent city conjured, in the teeth of the elements, from the northern swamps—is it not, as we read in the novel *A Raw Youth*, a purely imaginary and contrived conception? Is not its relation to the essence of Russia like that of a mirage to reality, of a deceitful mask to the true

---

[1]   "Man, if he'll be man in fact,
   Let him make eternal pact
   With his pious Mother Earth,
   With the soil that give him birth."
These words from Schiller's "Eleusinian Festival", the Credo of Dimitri Karamazov, are also Dostoevsky's Credo.

countenance? Is not the "St. Petersburg period" in Russian history the epoch of the great cleavage between actuality and appearance[1]; of a form of consciousness—presumptuous and illusory, because its roots in the nation are snapped—which withers up man's sense of his organic union with Mother Earth, and thus of the living reality of God and of the world?

This was approximately the verdict also of the Slavophils—to this extent, at least, they agreed with Dostoevsky. But they were content with delivering this verdict, and enquired no further: for they had no understanding of the antithesis in the Russian soul, whereas Dostoevsky had a full and penetrating comprehension of this antithesis, in its dialectical inevitability. Moreover, Dostoevsky shared Pushkin's love for the equivocal creation of that mighty magician, Peter the Great, with all its enigmatic and dangerous ambiguities.

It is inevitable that beneath the horse of the Bronze Rider in Senate Square there should writhe a serpent. (The Revolution is a logical corollary of Peter's work; and the anarchist Raskolnikov obviously belongs to the Revolution's serpent-brood.) Yet, without the Empire, would the Russian spirit have been able to develop into a universal spiritual power? Such was Pushkin's train of thought at the time when he wrote *The Bronze Rider*; and Dostoevsky swore by this master's words.

Literary-historical research has already pointed out the extent to which *Crime and Punishment* is derived from Pushkin's St. Petersburg tale *The Queen of Spades*. Dostoevsky himself emphasizes the deep significance of this tale: according to Dostoevsky, the character of its hero personifies the mood of the entire St. Petersburg period. There is, indeed, an unmistakable similarity

---

[1] *Cf.* the author's *Die Russische Idee.*

between the two works; but it is not merely the result of a simple imitation or reshaping of a literary model. The correspondence between them is a product of the identity of their basic mythical conceptions: the two tales are, as it were, variations on the same myth.

Pushkin's young officer, Hermann, a man of no family or fortune (in other words a plebeian and upstart, to his elegant and wealthy friends) and the hungry genius, the student Raskolnikov, are essentially akin; even though the former is a thoroughly selfish and loveless character, whereas the latter has a tender love for his mother and sister, who shyly and surreptitiously suffer deprivations in order to help him, and has a greater sense of grievance on their behalf than on his own.

Common to both are: social envy and personal ambition; an introverted and impenetrable nature, which seeks to shape day-to-day experiences into abstract patterns; the iron control of a passionate temperament by a will concentrated upon a single purpose; an almost pathological combination of unbridled fancifulness and cold calculation; moral scepticism; and, lastly, an unconscious magical urge to subjugate reality to their own demands— that which people who come in contact with either of these characters feel as something uncanny and daemonic in their natures.

Hermann, despite his modest, sober, strictly regulated mode of life, is generally regarded by his comrades as one who has "at least three crimes" upon his conscience; his comrades are repeatedly struck by his suddenly emergent resemblance to Napoleon. Raskolnikov's thoughts turn to Napoleon, as if drawn by a magnet: he admires Napoleon's daring, and his talent for crime.

The destinies of the two young men are also similar: both of them encounter—and this is where the mythical element enters—a terrifying old woman, whom they seek to rob of the treasure she is guarding; both incur the guilt of killing the Parca, and must suffer her posthumous revenge. For the mummy-like old Countess of the story, who takes with her to the grave the magic method of becoming rich, entrusted to her by Saint-Germain, is certainly the same deathless being who appears in the novel as an odious female money-lender.

What is the fatal Power that lurks behind these masks? Is not this female avenger, arising from the darkness, one of those earth-powers that can bring both woe and weal; that know the secrets of the Fates and keep subterranean riches under lock and key? Is she not an emissary of Mother Earth, rising in wrathful resistance against the over-audacious and presumptuous demands of visionary pride and rapacious high-handedness; against the wild attempt to annul by violence the decisions of eternal Themis?

If one seeks an explanation for her in the realm of myth, she can clearly be none other than a chthonian being. And the fact that she is, indeed, none other, is sufficiently expounded in Dostoevsky's variation on the theme; for clearly all his works are concerned with man's revolt against Mother Earth, the latter's resentment and her appeasement by the expiation demanded by her and made unto her.

3

The mythical element in the fundamental idea presented by *Crime and Punishment* is most plainly revealed in the mere plan of the work's central theme; which, without Dostoevsky's being aware of it—he is simply following popular tradition—might almost have served as the plot (*hypothesis*) for a play by Aeschylus, and can therefore be much better expressed in the technical language of ancient tragedy than by the concepts of modern ethics: the turbulent revolt of human arrogance and insolence (*hybris*) against the primitively-sacred decrees of Mother Earth; the preordained insanity of the evil-doer; the wrath of the Earth over the blood that has been shed; the ritual purification of the murderer—who is hunted by the Erinyes of spiritual anxiety, but is not yet repentant in the Christian sense—by the kissing of the Earth in the presence of the people assembled to try him; and the discovery, through suffering, of the right path (πάθει μάθος).

This kiss of submission, indeed, is the symbolic climax of the entire action, which is, as it were, over-shadowed by the invisible, gigantic figure of Gaia. It symbolizes the conflict and reconciliation between her and the proud son of Earth. The latter, aspiring to superhuman power, supposes that the more he alienates himself from the organic, the universal and the primitively real—whose vigour he has hitherto drawn from the all-nourishing mother-soil—the more he will exalt himself; and is thus driven to appease his hunger with the poisonous weeds of the wilderness that he creates within himself. ("The wilderness spreads woe unto him who carries the wilderness within him"—these are the very words of Nietzsche!) The hero of *Crime and Punishment* is guilty in the sight of Earth, and receives absolution through his expiation made unto Earth. When he has done this, then she, the patient and silent, who in her universal acceptance has taken his guilt upon herself, at the end reveals herself to the convalescent, in the manifestation of her boundless pastoral steppes, where still "the air of the Patriarchs" blows, and consoles and strengthens him.

How differently would the ambitious wiseacre have fared, had he acquired soon enough the wisdom of simple Brutus of the Roman saga; who, when told by the oracle that the *summum imperium* would go to him amongst those present who first should kiss his mother, at once fell down and touched the Earth with pious lips. *"Terram osculo contigit scilicet quod ea communis mater omnium mortalium esset."*—Livy, I, 56.

4

Crime and Punishment was Dostoevsky's first great revelation to the world, and the main pillar of his subsequent philosophy of life. It was a revelation of the mystic guilt incurred by the personality that shuts itself up in solitude, and for this reason drops out of the comprehensive unity of mankind, and thus also out of the sphere of influence of moral law. A formula had been found for negative self-determination by the individual: the name for it was—isolation. Raskolnikov's incarceration within himself, which was a result of the supreme decision of his free will (a will cut off from the universal whole), finds its final expression in the crime he commits. The sequence is not from crime to self-incarceration, but the converse: for from the latter arises the attempt to ensure the strength and autarky of the solitary personality—an attempt which, on the plane of external events, expresses itself as a crime.

It seemed to Dostoevsky that no symbolic action was expressive enough to convey a sense of the strange and almost incomprehensible—because so anomalous—spiritual condition of one who, like Cain, rejects God and man, shunning and fleeing all that lives. When Raskolnikov, after accepting the kindly gift that had been offered to him in error, later flung the small silver coin into the Neva, he knew that by this action he was severing the last bond between himself and mankind. Within the framework of the story we do not meet the rebel repentant of the murder he has committed, but merely one who refuses to endure the isolation which, under the mad illusion that it was a gauge of spiritual grandeur, he has voluntarily brought upon himself.

Worth noting is the dual character, deliberately emphasized by the author, of Raskolnikov's actions. On the one hand, all the circumstances, even the most trivial, array themselves in such a fashion that each separately and all collectively impel, adjure and force him to commit the deed that is apparently so contrary to his nature: a deed that results from some strange prompting from without, and is thereupon immediately regarded by Raskolnikov as an inexorable destiny. All his hesitation, all attempts to resist, are annulled by chance incidents, and conduce inevitably to the fatal step; as if his whole life were a torrent that with all its force surges irresistibly towards the huge precipice close ahead. On the other hand, Raskolnikov's whole environment appears to be in some sort a product of his imagination; and he who by chance puts the thought of murdering the old woman into his mind only gives utterance to something hidden and dormant within him. Raskolnikov himself creates this world of his. He is a magician of self-incarceration, and conjures up at will his miraculously created world of madness. He is also, however, the prisoner of his own phantom. He is saved by Sonia, who asks only one thing of her beloved: that he should acknowledge the reality of man and mankind outside of himself, and should solemnly declare his acceptance of this new and, to him, strange faith by an act of confession before all the people.[1]

Here we have an expression of the most important lesson that Dostoevsky learnt from inner experience during his exile. When, after his years in Siberia, he relates that he came to know the Russian people by sharing its ignominy and humiliation, and achieved union with it in suffering, and that in the same time he made himself acquainted with the Gospel, this confession has for us a double significance. There is no question here of a mere rapprochement between the "uprooted intellectual" of yesterday and the typical—indeed, according to Dostoevsky (*The House of the Dead*) the strongest and most significant—representatives of the Russian people's psyche, of the "people" in the empirical sense of the word: for this no Gospel would have been necessary. No, we are in the presence of something greater: for Dostoevsky the people itself is the all-unifying, universal human principle, which, in all its sinfulness and humiliation, embraces God and stands opposed to the isolated personality that is in conflict with God.

In all Dostoevsky's later dicta on the subject of the people it is equally evident that he is speaking of the

[1]*Cf.* the author's *Kluefte, ueber die Krisis des Humanismus* (Skythen-Verlag, Berlin), p. 36. "It is worth noting that the creator of *Crime and Punishment* agrees with Aeschylus (*cf.* the *Oresteia*) concerning the problem of purification after the shedding of blood: for the penitent's act of taking upon his shoulders the Cross held out to him by God Himself, of going into the market-place, kissing the earth and making full confession before all the people—is not all this essentially the same as Oedipus' abandoning his newly-attained throne, making a humble pilgrimage to Phoebus, and thus ratifying his inward purification by the verdict of the sacred national Areopagus?

"This mystic universalization of the conscience, this elevation of the universal human principle as a new power and a new value, such as do not reside in any single individual, to a level higher than any ever attainable by the individual's 'beautiful humanity'; and this view of the criminal as an apostate who is in need of reunion with the Whole: these things, it is plain, are not humanism."

people's supra-empirical essence, into which strike all the roots of the personality that has vanquished its solitude and become aware of its Ego as a limb of the universal body. And this Christian people, *spiritually* incorporated ln the Church and regarded by Dostoevsky as *one* soul, seems to him in a sense to merge into the concept of Earth as a mystical being; so that the apostate and rebel is, in Dostoevsky's view, a sinner not only against the Church, but also *contra naturam*.

5

The announcement of salvation through atonement—of the manner in which the personality discovers itself anew in God, by overcoming its illusory autarky of isolation—finds its climax in the Apotheosis and the cult of the Passion. In suffering man is truly united to all humanity. Be it even on the thief's cross, he experiences the mystery of contact with Christ. The sacramental significance, and thus the justification, of suffering resides in the fact that the victim, without knowing that he does so, suffers not only for himself, but also for others; that he not only himself experiences salvation through suffering, but also, whether he knows it or not, is saving others.

Even "the human louse"—as Raskolnikov calls the old female moneylender—atones through her suffering for some part of humanity's common sin. But he is none the less an evil-doer, that madman who conceives himself to be an instrument of the justice that he cannot comprehend: he does not alleviate, but only adds to the world's sorrow. The murder of the old woman becomes, in a manner unforeseen by Raskolnikov, also the murder of the simple, innocent Elizaveta. She who brings salvation to the murderer, the teacher of repentance, the meek-hearted Sonia, who becomes a prostitute in order to save her parents, brothers and sisters from starvation, is also a victim for the sins of others. In contrast to Elizaveta, however, Sonia is at the same time herself a great sinner; for, albeit to save others, she deliberately and overweeningly takes upon herself not only suffering, but also the curse of another's deed, by making it her own. In the sinner who expiates his sin by suffering, there is an antinomy of curse and salvation— unless it happens that love has not been extinguished within him; unless, like Svidrigalov, he has not become incapable of loving. For inability to love is Hell itself, as Zosima teaches; and he who is incapable of loving breaks away entirely from the partnership of all men in both sin and salvation.

The act of suffering finds a recognition appropriate to its dignity in Raskolnikov's prostration of himself before Sonia, and in the obeisance made by Father Zosima before Dimitri. This respect for suffering is the reason, according to Dostoevsky, why the Russian people adopt an attitude of deferential compassion towards "the unfortunate", as Russians call the criminal who is paying a just penalty.

The new theories of the irresponsibility of the criminal are to Dostoevsky objects of loathing: for they take from man his freedom and nobility, his divine dignity. No, the criminal must, and wants to, accept retribution for the act that expresses the metaphysical self-determination of his free will. It is unjust to deny to the criminal that responsibility that raises him above the beasts, and also to deny him the punishment that purifies him and gives him new being. Only the death-penalty, which forcibly curtails his Calvary of expiation, is to be condemned, since it is both hateful to God and also inhuman.

Nevertheless, every crime is not only a sin of the criminal, but also a sin of the community and of society: nobody has a right to say that he has no share in the guilt of the guilty. This opinion of Dostoevsky has its roots in the deepest and oldest strata of the national soul.

Whereas Raskolnikov's confession before all the people recalls the Orestes of Aeschylus, Dostoevsky's attitude towards the question of irresponsibility recalls the assessment of the guilt of Oedipus made in the tragedy by Sophocles. Oedipus—although unanimously acquitted by the latest researches into this perplexing and still not finally unriddled work—condemns himself. Why does he do so? He faces this dilemma: either he must regard himself as an automaton, a blind tool of fate—and therefore, in that he is unfree and irresponsible, also innocent; or else, disregarding the consequences and the apparent inconsistency, he must assert his freedom and responsibility, and thereby pass judgment upon himself.

There is an incomparable moral grandeur in the fact that Oedipus, who has solved the riddle of the Sphinx, and broken its spell, with the word "man", now condemns himself, the unwitting and unwilling criminal, in the name of man. This irrational solution of the problem, which has been set by the irrational beings who guide man's destiny,[1] turns the blind beggar, who on behalf of all mankind has given through his expiation a positive answer to the question of mankind's divinity, into a divine being and, in truth, a friend of the Eumenides.

----

[1]These irrational beings have a place in the fatalism of Sophocles—but not in the doctrines of Aeschylus, who has his own explanation of the curse laid upon Oedipus.

It is not Oedipus, in Dostoevsky's view, who is the criminal; yet he remains essentially the scapegoat of the Old Testament, the scapegoat that carries the sins of the people, the φαρμακὸς of the ancient Greeks. Similarly, in the case of Raskolnikov, the will of the many, which is directed towards the elimination of the repulsive old woman, finds a fulcrum in the free consent of this sick man, who is sick because he is in revolt against Heaven and Earth.

In *The Brothers Karamazov*, Dostoevsky, with Mephisto-phelian acumen, stresses the fact that the inhabitants of the little town, who were so enraged by the murder of old Karamazov, secretly hoped that the murderer would prove to be his son.

These indications given us by Dostoevsky help us to understand the dark meaning of Raskolnikov's terrible dream, and to recognize its significance within the plan of the novel. Raskolnikov dreams of a pitiful old nag that is being tortured to death by a jeering, wild and drunken mob. Who bears the guilt of this disgusting act of cruelty? Obviously not only the wildly excited owner of the unfortunate animal, who is swaggeringly eager to amuse the company, but also every individual of those who in sheer wantonness add to a load that is already beyond the animal's strength.

Which, then, of the characters in the novel resembles this obscure victim? Sonia alone? No, also her father and mother—and Elisaveta. And not only they: also the murdered old moneylender, and above all the murderer himself, who has been condemned, or has condemned himself, to accomplish that which the collective will demanded.

Already in *Crime and Punishment* Dostoevsky discovers, to his horror, the truth which he later on expresses as a dogma: the truth of the guilt of all men, for all men and for everything. This dreadful discovery opens before him still another abyss, both terrifying and illumining: he begins to apprehend that all humanity is—one man. *Omnes unum.* (*St. John* xiv, 20.)

Chapter III

THE STRANGER

I

HAVING indicated, in *Crime and Punishment*, the main criterion of distinction between the way of good (that is, the way of practical recognition of universal human oneness, founded in God, as a spiritual reality) and the way of evil (that is, the way of inward isolation, of overshadowing self-will and of Deicide), Dostoevsky in his later works develops and deepens this fundamental conception by depicting it in a great variety of forms, in the dichotomy of particular individuals, of philosophical attitudes and of destinies.

At the same time he regards it as urgently necessary to present, if not a finally complete image, at least a rough indication of the positive human type that follows the former of the two ways: the type that, despite the law of life that separates and isolates men, nevertheless gives living reality to the principle of all-embracing community and unity. Searching the world of literature for a proto-type of the man of goodwill, Dostoevsky lingers with special affection over the immortal work of Cervantes.[1]

---

[1]"The idea of my novel," he writes in a letter about his work on *The Idiot*, "is the old one that I have always favoured, but it is so difficult that hitherto I have not dared to carry it out. The main object of the novel is: to present in positive form a really good man. There is nothing in the world more difficult to do than this, but especially nowadays. Beauty is an ideal; yet neither our ideal nor that of civilized Europe is even in the remotest degree perfected. . . . Of all the beautiful figures in Christian literature, Don Quixote is the most complete. Don Quixote, however, is beautiful only because he is at the same time absurd."

In fact, the positive type that Dostoevsky sought must either present a countenance of perfect holiness, amazingly transcending the limitations of humanity—but such a countenance would be the subject of a mystery, not of a realistic life story; or it must produce a tragi-comic effect—by reason of its discordance or, one might say, its incommensurability with its human environment, combined with its inward oneness with this environment in virtue of the common law of life that governs both.

Here we find the first impulse towards the creation of *The Idiot*. Regarded from the standpoint of literary genealogy, Don Quixote is undoubtedly one of the ancestors of Prince Myshkin. An essential feature is common to both: their Platonism and Platonic Eros. Don Quixote is above all a devoted admirer of Dulcinea, the "tender" womanly beauty, "bewitched by the Powers of Evil"; a beauty that is spiritually real, but in the empirical world is hidden behind the unworthy mask of coarse physicality. Don Quixote perceives the mystical essence of Dulcinea by means of an inward illumination—much as Pushkin's "Poor Knight" perceives the Mother of God:

> [1]Lived a knight once, poor and simple,
>   Pale of face with glance austere,
> Spare of speech, but with a spirit
>   Proud, intolerant of fear.
> He had had a wondrous vision:
>   Ne'er could feeble human art
> Gauge its deep, mysterious meaning,
>   It was graven on his heart.
> And since then his soul had quivered
>   With an all-consuming fire,
> Never more he looked on women,
>   Speech with them did not desire.

---

[1]Translated from the Russian original as quoted in *The Idiot* by Constance Garnett.

But he dropped his scarf thenceforward.
  Wore a chaplet in its place,
And no more in sight of any
  Raised the visor from his face.
Filled with purest love and fervour,
  Faith which his sweet dream did yield,
In his blood he traced the letters
  A.M.D.[1] upon his shield.
When the Paladins proclaiming
  Ladies' names as true love's sign,
Hurled themselves into the battle
  On the plains of Palestine,
Lumen Coeli, Sancta Rosa!
  Shouted he with flaming glance,
And the fury of his menace
  Checked the Mussulman's advance.
Then returning to his castle
  In far distant countryside,
Silent, sad, bereft of reason,
  In his solitude he died.

It is not an accident that Dostoevsky, whilst also mentioning Don Quixote, describes this ballad, with its brilliant penetration into the depths of the medieval soul, as a leitmotif of Myshkin's Platonism—in so far, at least, as this is understood by Aglaya, who is in love with Myshkin and is actuated by jealousy when she makes him the butt of her mockery.

Nevertheless, Myshkin is neither Don Quixote nor the Poor Knight. In creating his hero—a "positive" character, yet necessarily ridiculous in men's eyes—Dostoevsky does not abide by his chosen literary example. With poetic intuition he examines the innermost essence of the type personified in his hero; and, as usually happens

---

[1] *Ave Mater Dei.* In *The Idiot* the poem is deliberately misquoted by Aglaya, *N.F.B.* being substituted for *A.M.D.*

88

before the growth of a great poetic conception, he finds its native soil—which never denies its strengthening sustenance to any truly original work—in obscure memories of ancient myth.

This eccentric, unlike all other men; he who, as it were, descends upon other men from unknown heights—heights that he himself can scarcely remember; who, naïvely proclaiming his own inner law, a law that can be measured by no human standards, meekly and joyfully carries the sign of his royal anointment; who, without being recognized by men, speaks with them simply and trustfully, as if they, too, were anointed like himself; who is infinitely close to something hotly desired but forgotten in men's souls, and yet, despite the benign and miraculous power that issues from him, remains alien to them: this eccentric, this stranger, is no longer known to folklore as a shining god come down to earth, but, instead, as a hero—that is to say, a godlike man who must suffer and die.

Prince Myshkin, who never knew woman, is no longer the Parsifal of the original, Celtic legend, but the "pure fool" of later, medieval legend. At the same time, however, he is the Ivan-the-Tsarevich of the old Russian tale; the simple and true-hearted one; he who instinctively knows and foretells; the worker of wonders; the friend of animals, who reads the soul of Nature like an open book; he who lives like a somnambulist, and indeed betrays signs of somnolence in his daily life (compare the meeting of Myshkin and Aglaya at which the latter finds her lover asleep on a garden bench); he who is led by destiny to his appointed throne, and in the light of a superhuman glory is suddenly surprised and carried off by death.

2

Prince Myshkin is, above all, the type of a spirituality that descends, that seeks the Earth: rather a spirit that assumes flesh than a man who rises to the spiritual. All his glory lies behind him, in his past: both the glory of his family's historic name, and also that transcendent, supra-terrestrial, harmonious blessedness, that very spectacle of beauty whose shapeless memory blossoms (as the poet of the "blue flower" says) "like a Heav'n of nameless sweetness, evermore within his soul".

This preponderance of the Platonic *anamnesis* over the sense of reality is just what makes him at once a fool and a wise seer amongst men. There are moments when this anamnesis flares up terrifyingly within him, as if the curtain had been rent that separates the external world from that other, earlier world. At such moments this anamnesis dazzles, convulses and consumes the soul, just as the suddenly unveiled splendour of Zeus consumes Semele; and yet at the same time it conveys a fleeting sense of unutterable bliss and redemption. These are the moments when Myshkin succumbs to his attacks of epilepsy. The primitive memory is so strong in him that until his twenty-fourth year he cannot adjust himself to this world of ours, and seems an "Idiot".

In him we have a soul that has plunged from that "place beyond the skies" (ἐπουράνιος τόπος) described by Plato, where, with the gods, men unborn contemplate the forms of eternal beauty. What, then, caused his earthward plunge? Doubtless a passionate longing for Earth and for earthly incarnation. Myshkin is in love with Earth, and sees in her something that he has beheld in the celestial regions: he sees her as she eternally *is* in God. Hence his daily experience of Paradise, his direct perception of Nature in her original purity, which she retains for all time in her eternal essence and her sacred depths.

Myshkin sees that over Nature's bright face flit the shadows of sorrow; but just as he loves the "perfect" beauty of Nastasia Filippovna's lovely face all the more because of the marks of suffering upon it, so, too, he holds that in Nature even her sorrow cannot mar the pristine form that lives within her. For even suffering, as seen by Dostoevsky, contains within it a sanctifying and purifying force.

Myshkin is by no means an idealist in the style of Raskolnikov, for example; he is entirely made up of memory of all that he has seen, he has a sunshine-clear, divinely illumined eye for all that is visible.

Other men, of course, cannot remember the things that are stored in Myshkin's memory, and do not see what he sees: they have no choice, therefore, but to take him for a fool. For some reason, however, it never occurs to anybody to call him a fancymonger. Indeed, he preaches no ideology; and what though he measures human relationships by his own peculiar standards, he gives evidence of a wholly direct and realistic feeling in his understanding of human beings, human passions, compulsions and calculations. So unerringly does he read the motives of men's actions, so sober is his appraisal of matters of fact, that gradually they come to regard the "Idiot" as a sage. It is characteristic of Myshkin that, in a conversation in which he is expected to make an avowal of spiritual values, he "laughs good-naturedly" and calls himself "a materialist".

The fact is that all the secret suffering of this soul, which does not achieve incarnation, arises from the incompleteness of this incarnation. This is also the reason why Myshkin, when living in a village in the Swiss mountains, loved to engross himself in contemplation of the waterfall behind the village; and also why, even as he rejoiced in the waterfall, he felt so "restless and full of yearning". Was it not the same irrepressible yearning that compelled him to descend from the familiar, other-worldly heights to an Earth shrouded in the dark veils of sorrow?

Why is he not allowed to become completely a son of Earth? Why is he denied complete incarnation? Why must he remain for all eternity a spirit that has strayed to Earth—a stranger, a visitor from unknown regions? This man to whom beauty brings both happiness and martyrdom; who knows that beauty is a riddle he cannot solve, but knows none the less surely that "it is beauty that will save the world"; who with his clear vision beholds the unveiled splendour of Nature—this man complains: what is this feast, this everlasting festival, which has no end, which has allured him since his earliest childhood, and in which he can never, never fully share? He feels all too bitterly that there is no place for him at this feast, and this only makes him love life all the more.

The love of life—of life for its own sake, and not merely of the joys and pleasures of existence—a love, that is to say, that can even survive the fiery test of suffering—is, in Dostoevsky's eyes, a great and positive spiritual value. It is this love of life, and this alone, that continues to sustain and animate the spiritually half-dead Ivan Karamazov. "It is beautiful to be alive; do you love this life?" This question of Dostoevsky's *Laudlady* is the question addressed to man by the soul of the universe.

The first love of the youthful Myshkin—when he awoke in Switzerland from his state of dim insensibility, and for the first time looked at the world about him—

was, so he himself tells us, an ass. Between this ass and himself there was, in fact, a double bond: not only the reputation for stupidity that human injustice had attached to both of them, but also the disinterested, stubborn heroism of that tough patience which arises from love of life, from the love of life that distinguishes the martyr. Perhaps this last characteristic was one of the reasons why, in the old orgiastic rites, the ass enjoyed a quite especial respect.

3

It must have been some ecstatic experience—undergone, perhaps, during his trance on the place of execution—that gave rise to the conception, which moved Dostoevsky so deeply, of a Paradise on Earth, a Paradise that is close to us and yet unrecognized. It would instantly reveal itself to us, if only we had the courage of the pure heart, the courage to open our eyes and see it.

At the period of *The Idiot* this conception appears to be still quite naïve; and only later, in the utterances of Father Zosima, does it acquire some sort of theological foundation. Be that as it may, however, it is remarkable in how mythical a form Dostoevsky presents his poetical perception of those states of consciousness which are described in the language of the New Testament as "peace" and "the Kingdom of Heaven within man". True love of life, as an ontological virtue, is the best soil for these heavenly growths; whereas the inner forces that make them grow are awareness of complicity in the guilt for the world's sorrow, and the heart's knowledge of the all-redeeming value of suffering.

Since I know myself to be guilty in the sight of all

men, then not only have I long since forgiven them that have trespassed against me, but I have also attained the Grace-given consolation of an inner certainty. Thus I enjoy in anticipation the sense of that general reconciliation which, in the conversation between Alyosha and Ivan concerning the tears of childhood, is revealed to be an essential condition of Paradise, but which human-sentimental judgment deems impossible. If I do this, then my suffering is made light for me, because with it I pay a part of the common debt of guilt, which is also my debt. Then, too, the suffering of others, endured for me and for all, is revealed to me in the revolving circle of love as a love-offering by the sufferers and the birth-travail of a rapturous bliss. Such a bliss is the certain result of this actual, what though unconscious, victory won in the Kingdom of Heaven, where all are one, over the law of human isolation.

The sense of Paradise on Earth is seen by Dostoevsky as a sure token of a state of Grace. Zosima's brother, who died in early youth, says on his deathbed serenely to his mother: "Don't cry, Mother, life is a paradise and we are all in paradise, but we won't see it, if we could we should have Heaven on earth next day."[1] Even the "mysterious visitor" of the young Zosima declares: "Heaven is hidden within all of us . . . here it lies hidden within me now, and if I will it, it will be revealed to me tomorrow and for all time."[1] It is his sense of oppression by an unexpiated crime that prevents him from willing it. So soon, however, as he has become reconciled with his conscience, and with men, by means of public confession, he does, in fact, experience the longed-for state, and departs from life in peace.

Myshkin, in *The Idiot*, has the same awareness.

---

[1] Translation from the Russian original by Constance Garnett.

He has it in a form peculiar to himself, and it was at one time for him a daily experience: and this is just what makes him unlike other men and yet binds him to them. From time to time he is consoled by the gracious light that illumines the vale of woe through which he is passing.

The perception of Paradise on Earth, the sense of immortality in every instant, the April of earthly life; the happiness of existence, all these help to bring Myshkin into close and direct touch with children, and to give him a spiritual kinship with them.

Dostoevsky believes that love of children, joy in them and close and direct contact with them, is a sign of a special state of Grace. Myshkin and Alyosha have it in common.

Dostoevsky's metaphysics of childhood deserve particular study. The child is the central point of his doctrine concerning the world and concerning man. In *The Brothers Karamazov* he symbolically depicts the tragic destiny of Russia, when he describes the prophetic dream that came to Dimitri (Mitya) on the threshold of his martyrdom. In this dream Russia is seen as a burnt-out village, sunk in misery and despair. As Mitya drives through it, starving mothers hold out their babies to him. Full of pity and horror, Mitya enquires in his dream what is the origin of all this unhappiness; and the only answer he gets is the phrase, endlessly reiterated: "the child is weeping". This pierces his heart: "the child is weeping" is the source of the world's sorrow. The world's unforgivable sin is the sin against children.

Dostoevsky believes that always there are hosts of souls descending from Heaven to Earth, still retaining their celestial memories and bearing within them the possibility of a sudden transformation of Earth into

Heaven—if only the gift they bear remains inviolate, unsquandered and unprofaned. They approach human beings with childish trustfulness, bearing the glad tidings that at any moment Heaven may be made manifest. But men offend and corrupt them, men infect them with their sinfulness, men change the young herbs that spring from the Heavenly seed into bitter hemlock.

"Children must grow in gardens," Dostoevsky writes in his *Journal of an Author*. And he adds: "In the future, even factories will be surrounded by gardens." With almost morbid eagerness, he constantly repeats the injunction: "Do not torment the children, do not soil or corrupt them."

Myshkin, like Alyosha, is a child when he is among children. And in the depths of his being, although his thoughts plumb the nature of evil, he remains always a child. Thus, in the words of the Gospel, he bears within him the light of the Kingdom of Heaven. His meeting with the children occurs at the beginning of his conscious life; and the only practical achievement of which he is capable on earth is the rescue of the Swiss village girl, Marie, and the conversion of her small persecutors.

4

But this practical achievement is only the first step towards the fulfilment of a great and mysterious task, which is represented in myth as the mission of Him who comes down upon earth. The Heavenly emissary, whatever his name may be, must deliver the world's soul from the bondage of an evil enchantment. He must free Andromeda from her chains, abduct Eurydice or Alcestis from Hades, waken the Sleeping Beauty. This is the liberator for whom waits the "Landlady" ensorcelled by Murin; for whom waits the female cripple in *The Possessed* (for alone, of her own strength, she could never have walked); and for whom waits likewise that Beauty who comes down upon earth to save the world ("it is beauty that will bring the world salvation"), but then, like the Ashtaroth of the Gnostics, becomes imprisoned in matter and desecrated—she, the "Eternal Female" herself, who is depicted, in *The Idiot*, by the symbolic figure of Nastasia Filippovna. It seems as though Dostoevsky's portrait of her was modelled on the Sistine Madonna at Dresden, of which he was especially fond. It is not without significance that Aglaya, in the parody of *The Poor Knight* that she directs against the young Prince, replaces the mystic sign, "A(ve) M(ater) D(ei)", or "A(ve) M(aria) D(eipara)", by the initials of her rival.

Myshkin's first sight of Nastasia Filippovna's picture comes upon him like a stroke of lightning, and suddenly wakens a memory: it is as though he had seen Nastasia Filippovna's eyes in a dream. Surely he has seen her before, at some time? She, too, remembers that they have at some time already met. In Myshkin's eyes her beauty is perfect. "Nastasia Filippovna is perfection, even though she is thin and pale."[1] "I cannot endure Nastasia Filippovna's face, I am afraid of her face," he confesses. However beautiful Aglaya may be, for him she is only "almost as beautiful" as Nastasia Filippovna. Nevertheless, the feeling that the latter arouses in Myshkin is not love, but only a boundless admiration and a boundless pity.

It is disastrous for Nastasia Filippovna and for Myshkin that both of them are beings who have come down from on high; for Myshkin's love is directed

---

[1] Translation from the Russian original by Constance Garnett.

towards the Earth, and longs for a figure that is born of Earth and rises from Earth to meet him, not for one that descends towards Earth.

Nastasia Filippovna has a rival: the physically blooming and glorious Aglaya ("the festively resplendent"). Myshkin cannot help being drawn to her earthly beauty, just as he is drawn, in his own words, to "the Feast of life on earth"; for the very reason that his own embodiment in the flesh is incomplete, and he longs for a deeper incarnation. Thus is sealed the tragic guilt of the heavenly messenger, his metaphysical downfall, his fatal mania, and also the fundamental cause of the sickness that again attacks him. For Earth cannot, in that aspect of her which he loves in Aglaya, answer in her entirety to the call of the Word within him; and Aglaya loves him in such a manner as to desire rather to entice him and enfold him in her primitive darkness than to attain freedom through him. It is not without cause that she is at length submerged in the deceit and blackness of life. In Myshkin is repeated the story of Don Quixote: his light falls upon unyielding, sluggish, resistant matter, but proves powerless to reshape it, so that he becomes no more than a figure of comedy.

5

As a result of this disastrous conflict in Myshkin's soul, and his betrayal of Heaven, Nastasia Filippovna perishes. She knows that in his person her redeemer, her saviour stands before her ("Did I not bring him here by my own longing?" she says herself); but the hand he holds out towards her proves to be the feeble hand of a man who has started away and stopped. Why cannot he turn his gaze from Aglaya? Even if, as Rogozhin remarks, his pity is stronger than his love, nevertheless this boundless, divine pity makes terms in his heart with another, undefined yet overpowering feeling. Is this latter feeling love? No, it is only the lure of Earth, which works upon his soul with primitive force, and finds (for "he can take no part in the Feast of Life") no outlet or expression.

Aglaya, for her part, knows this dichotomy all too well; for at moments, when, as it seems, he has surrendered completely to her spell, there appears before him his "intangible vision", the image of her rival, and draws his soul unto herself. "He turned his head," Dostoevsky relates, "looked at her, glanced into her black eyes which flashed at the moment with a light he could not understand" (Nastasia Filippovna he understands with all his being; earthly desire, on the other hand, is beyond his understanding), "tried to smile at her, but immediately, as though forgetting her, turned his eyes to the right" (Aglaya is sitting on a garden bench to his left—thus, according to popular belief, on the side of the spirit of temptation) "and again began watching the *unearthly apparition*"[1].

What, then, of the disastrous resistance that Nastasia Filippovna offers to all Myshkin's stubborn appeals? Is it merely the refusal of a proud woman to accept the dole of pity that is offered her in place of love? Far from it! The impulses of her soul are infinitely more complex and nobler, her view of the deliverer calling her is deeper and broader. Behind the mask of haughtiness that she holds up to the world like a shield, she is profoundly humble, and in any case certainly cannot be counted amongst those "proud women" whose natures Dostoevsky explored, with all their refinements, and whom

---

[1]Translation from the Russian original by Constance Garnett.

he by no means admired: women who, in their beloved, do not love the man himself, but the creation of their own desires, and even at the moment of utter self-abnegation are basically selfish.

The mortification that Nastasia Filippovna feels is grief for the desecration of her sacred dignity as a woman—nay, more: for the violation and murder of her soul. Her assumed arrogance, her deliberately challenging behaviour, the self-torture of her feigned shamelessness— all these things are nothing but a mask behind which she seeks to hide her despair of rescue and redemption. Nearer the surface of her soul, emotions pursue each other in wild fluctuation: mortification and revolt, sullenness and shame, contempt for human beings, hatred of pity, even jealousy. This last emotion is conquered by the argument, worked out with truly feminine casuistry, that the Prince could be happy with Aglaya, whereas an unequal and fanciful marriage between "a person like him" and herself, a woman of ill repute, would be his ruin: far better, therefore, that she herself should perish; her destiny wills it, and it serves her right. Yet her deepest and truest feelings, which arise from an instinctive intuition into the mystery of her encounter with Myshkin, are the products of a religious humility, an honourable repentance for her sinfulness, and a tender, motherly compassion.

Her deferential awe in the presence of him whom she recognizes as the visitor from Heaven is as intense as her remorseful awareness of her impurity, of her fall. This awareness flames up within her and consumes her as soon as her eyes meet Myshkin's forgiving gaze. No, she is not "worthy to dream of him". It would better become her to wash his feet and dry them with her hair. How should she, the sinner, dare to call him her spouse?

"He's the one she fears most," remarks the intelligent wag, Lebediev, "and that is the secret."[1]

At the same time, however, she sees his childish helplessness, which provokes a maternal love in her; she feels an agonizing pity for him; she has a sense of his anguish and a premonition of his downfall. In spirit she detains him in her arms and sheds tears over him, like the Mother of God in paintings entitled "Pietà". She must have no earthly contact with him. Her *path of sacrifice* leads her to the accursed house of Rogozhin, just as Cassandra's path led her to the accursed halls of the Atreidae—to the knife, to the execution which she has deserved, and which is to redeem her.

6

Dostoevsky has in this work dropped anchor in such depths that he cannot completely raise it again. To clear his vessel, he had to cut more than one cable. Only in part could he give artistic form to what he had beheld: he himself says in his letters that he "has not given expression to a tenth of what he intended"; yet he adds that he "loves to this day his miscarried"—that is to say, incompletely expressed—"ideas".

What he has succeeded in expressing is incomparable in its power and inspiration. But so other-worldly was his conception that he could not extract its entire content, or completely express it within the limits of artistic awareness. Had he been able to do so, all men would have cried out, in the words of that Barbarian King who had enquired of his guest concerning the destiny of the human soul: "Has not the seer taught our hearts again to know whence the swallow flew, which for a moment

---

[1] Translation from the Russian original by Constance Garnett.

appeared in the firelight of this bright-lit company, and what it was that drove her back into her native darkness?" Because Dostoevsky has not been able to do this, *The Idiot*, as a work, must be regarded—for the very reason that it is permeated by the primitive elements of myth—as incomplete. It may be, too, that the interlocking of various mythical themes made it more difficult for him to provide the final artistic clarification. In *The Idiot* we see how the myth—the living soul of the novel—sometimes breaks out far beyond the limits of its material shell and shatters it, without finding complete expression in the physical aspects of the life the novel portrays; so that the reader who follows the story under these aspects can scarcely discern the myth.

Everything in this novel is enigmatic, capable of many interpretations; this is true even of the figure—permeated by an extraordinary, enlivening force, yet veiled in dark mystery—of the debauchee and barbarian Rogozhin. The impotent redeemer and the murderer who performs the act of redemption have a positively magnetic mutual relationship: where one is, there, invariably and inexorably, is the other. Each feels, unconsciously but with absolute inner certainty, the other's approach. Each without wishing to do so, draws the other to him. It is as if each of them became flesh and blood on earth only at the other's call, at the call of his antipode and twin. As rivals they duplicate each other, like "the enemy brothers", although they present themselves as beings of two different worlds that have nothing in common: for who would suppose that the soul of Parfyon Rogozhin ($\pi\alpha\rho\theta\acute{\epsilon}\nu\iota\sigma$—the virginal) could be the sister-soul of Myshkin, that carrier of the consecration of the Spirit? Even allowing for the crudity of the material shell that encases the soul, and for the soul's

capacity for deep and desperate immersion in the dark
chaos of unruly passions that daemonically overshadow
its failing inner light and make it greedy and ruthless—
even allowing for these, who could imagine a spiritual
sisterhood between these two characters? The one has
not attained full incarnation; the other can scarcely carry
his earthly load. The one descends to Earth; the other,
by his faith (tried by doubt) in Christ's victory, and by the
joyfully accepted expiation, walks towards the light. Yet
in a mysterious way they need and complete each other.

We may suppose that to Dostoevsky the two characters
conjointly represent, in their duality-in-unity, the
synthesis of the Russian soul. The Prince, of an ancient
Russian family, whom even his upbringing abroad, in
the West (an allusion to the Western culture of Russia's
higher social strata) cannot detach from the roots
of his people; and the other, bound to him in blood-
brotherhood, the representative of the obscure masses
of the people: both men have the same creed and the
same mystical view of life; or, rather, the same clairvoyance. That is why they both in the same measure
recognize the metaphysical countenance of Nastasia
Filippovna (ἀνάστασις—resurrection). Is it, then, surprising that they should become brothers in spirit,
should exchange their crosses, and, although rivals, love
each other like sons of one father? Both feel drawn to
the same woman, for whom they have been designated
by destiny. Which of the two will win her: he who gives
reality to the principle of life, and even under ordeal by
fire proves himself capable of living; or he whom life
rejects and repudiates? The one claims the bride by right
of the boundless love which he, as a son of Earth, has
for the heavenly Beauty that descends to redeem the
world; the other claims her in his right as a son of

Heaven filled with divine pity for the martyrdom of the Beauty whom the world has deformed and reviled.

He whose love is no compassion, becomes compassionate when he releases Nastasia by the sacrificial knife; and, on that fatal night when the whole action has come to a head, the performer of the sacrifice yields Nastasia, who, as it were, no longer belongs to Earth, over to his other, better Ego, his spiritual brother. The latter, knowing nothing of the bloody deed that has been wrought, stations himself, at the murderer's bidding, beside the virginal-nuptial bed, close by his murdered bride, who is hidden by a curtain, whilst Parfyon lies on the other side. This shattering scene is filled with a silent horror that carries the soul away in a whirlwind of madness.

What is the legend repeated—in a remote echo, as it were, and amidst hoary ruins—by these broken sentences, these muffled cries of two entranced beings for whom the world has been thrown off its hinges and all bindings and bonds of existence have been relaxed and cast aside? Where before have we seen these two setting out on a barge, accompanied by a woman, upon the boundless and benighted sea of the unknown—and returning alone, without her, to the shore? Where have we heard these confused and incoherent laments, born of the feverish delirium of jealousy and despair, for the Beauty who languishes in the bonds of Earth and is delivered by death before she can be delivered?

The reader will remember the "Night Voyage" in Heinrich Heine's *Romancero*:

> The sea was high, the half-moon peeped
> Through dark clouds timidly
> And, as we mounted on the skiff,
> Our company numbered three.

THE STRANGER

The water splashed to the beat of the oar
   With dull monotony;
White-crested waves came surging up
   And spattered us all three.

She stood on the skiff, so slim, so pale,
   And so unflinchingly,
Like a marble statue from foreign lands,
   Diana's image, she.

And now the moon is entirely hid,
   The wind blows cold and dree:
High, of a sudden, above our heads
   A cry rings piercingly.

'Twas the cry of a white and spectral gull:
   Like a warning prophecy
It rang, that sinister, evil shriek,
   And we were afraid, all three.

Am I a-fevered? Is yonder a ghost?
   Or some midnight phantasy?
Am I mocked by a dream? Ah, what a dream,
   What ghastly buffoonery!

Ghastly buffoonery! I dream
   That salvation comes through me;
That 'tis I who bear the heavy Cross
   With patient loyalty.

Poor Beauty, she is sore distressed:
   'Tis I who shall set her free
From shame and sin, from pain and want
   And the world's obscenity.

Beauty distressed, ah, do not shrink
   From this bitter pharmacy:
'Tis I myself who award thee death,
   Though my heart shall die with thee.

FREEDOM AND THE TRAGIC LIFE

Ah, buffoonery, cruel dream,
  Madness and lunacy!
The night's agape, the ocean shrieks—
  O God, ah, succour me!

Ah, succour me, all-merciful God!
  What is't that falls in the sea?
Oh, hear, oh, hear, all-merciful God,
  Adonai, hear my plea!

The sun arose, we put for land;
  There was blossom on every tree!
And as we descended from the skiff,
  Two were our company.

Part III

Theological Aspect

Part III

Theological Aspect

(θεολογούμενα)

O voi che avete gl'intelletti sani,
Mirate la dottrina che s'asconde
Sotto il velame degli versi strani.

"OYE of sound understanding, consider well the
doctrine that lurks behind the veil of strange
poetry," says Dante (*Inferno*, IX, 61). Although his lines
may seem as uncommon as the clothes of a visitor from
abroad, yet from under the pilgrim's garb shines the
truth of the Church's teaching. "Reader, sharpen here
your vision of the truth, for the veil is now so fine that
indeed it is easy to pierce,"[1] so Dante writes in another
passage. And throughout *The Divine Comedy* appears—
beneath the everlasting snow of mystical perceptions,
amidst the colourfully changing cloud-screen of symbolic
images—the unshakable rock of scholastic theology,
whose name, in the language of St. Thomas Aquinas,
is "Sacra Doctrina".

We are equally entitled to speak—*mutatis mutandis*—of
a "doctrine" propounded by Dostoevsky. Both writers
make it "the end of the whole and of each part"—we
quote Dante's words concerning his own work—"to

---

[1]Aguzza qui, lettor, ben gli occhi al vero,
Che il velo e ora ben tanto sottile,
Certo, che'l trapassar dentro e leggiero.

—*Purgatorio*, VIII, 19.

remove the living, whilst their lives are still here on earth, from the state of misery, and to lead them to the state of bliss. Both see the way to this end in religious truth. Both have "taken the veil of poetry from the hand of truth". For both, poetic vision is a covering through which the gaze can penetrate, so that behind it is revealed the secret of other worlds. Cultural environment induces Dostoevsky towards contemplation, Dante towards defence of the Church's teaching. Dante dispenses comfort to the faithful; Dostoevsky seeks to rescue those whose roots in religion have been severed. But both alike are teachers of the Faith; both peer down into the deepest chasms of evil; both accompany the sinful and redemption-seeking soul along the difficult paths of its ascent; both perceive the blessedness of the divine harmony; both seek to show, each to his own nation, its historic task in the light of the Christian ideal.

To this extent they have traits in common; but, against this background of common aims, the contrast between these two religiously minded artists stands out all the more clearly. The difference between them as preachers of the Faith is by no means confined to the contrast between the views and methods of him who takes his stand upon the fact of revelation—a fact, for him, generally acknowledged, and as undeniable by the reader as by himself—and those of him who, although he himself possesses sure knowledge of this fact, does not assume that others have, as a matter of course, the same certainty. Dante's teaching is epically complete like the Church's dogma; as rigid as the order of Hell; as immutable—amidst all the mighty stress of spiritual experience—as the heavenly Rose that drinks the light of countless souls. Dostoevsky's apologetics, on the other hand, are essentially dynamic and tragic.

Dante is, from the outset, one of the saved: that is why he is led by a true and sure Guide. Dostoevsky is, from the outset, "numbered amongst the evil-doers". In his daily life he continually experiences within himself the responsibility of each for all, "the guilt of each in the sight of all, on behalf of all, and for everything"—and, with this guilt, necessarily also the saving power of Grace. A herald of the pious tidings of redemption, he does not hold aloof from the host of the outcast and spiritually blind, but dwells in their midst. As sorely tormented as any of these, or as the first renegade from Faith and rebel against God, he seeks, in the darkness of his own soul and the souls of others, that light which no darkness can quench; and when, for a brief moment, he beholds it, he calls out to the others the news of what he has seen. And again, when all is once more swallowed up by the dark, he once more seeks access to the source of this light; and whenever he sees it anew, he hastens to announce it to those who remain "in the night and the shadow of death"—to those dwellers in Plato's "Cave" who know not the light of the sun. He has no other guide than the countenance of Christ, which he has once seen and loved.

Thus, with this vision in his soul, Dostoevsky passes like a sleep-walker along the edges of yawning, sinister chasms. Two souls dwell in his breast, and each is aware of the conditions of its growth.

> While the trunk drinks the bright air,
>   Plunge the tap-roots into Night;
> Stygian waters have a share
>   In the growth of Ether's might.

Dostoevsky has long since made his choice: his surety and pledge for it is the figure of Christ shining upon his path. He knows the path "that leads to life", and also the path "that leads to destruction". But his relationship with the Inferno is different from Dante's: the Hell that he vanquishes is a dispersed part of his own self, and the flame of Purgatory sears him with unending torments. His cry to God is ever "out of the depths I cry to thee" (*de profundis clamavi*). No signs reach him from a Beatrice awaiting him in Heaven. Only the "holy sickness" at moments lifts before him the curtain over the entrance to Paradise.

How is religious truth revealed to this strange apologist? He explores the human soul in its sickness, in its cataclysms, in the depths of ultimate self-awareness that these convulsions disclose. Or, at other times, he portrays souls that, from birth onwards and by the law of their own natures, involuntarily, and indeed unconsciously, reverse the worldly-wise precept "primum vivere, deinde philosophari"; souls whose entire behaviour—nay, their existence and sojourn in this world—is determined by what is commonly described as the "search for the meaning of life"; that is to say, by the decision to answer the fundamental question of whether, in Dostoevsky's words, they will "accept" as inevitable the world that presents itself before them, or will "refuse to accept this world".

Dostoevsky confronts those who search for the meaning of life with the basic dilemma of human existence. In their moments of spiritual crisis they see before them, as if illumined by a flash of lightning, the only two ways open to mankind: the way of acknowledgment of God, and the way of refusal to acknowledge Him.

By its fruits ye shall know the truth. Analysis of the decisive self-determination—which can consist only in

Svid lures Dunya into a delib. trap — to is at love but demo of relat. between reason and sensuality — (Kirghiz on a lower level)

THEOLOGICAL ASPECT   Dunya's behind a

reasonable
sin

an unconditional affirmation, or an equally unconditional denial, of the personality's own metaphysical existence and ontological value—may indicate how the act of faith is possible. The psychologist and mystic is supported by a powerful dialectic: from the premise either of an affirmation or of a denial of religious truth, this dialectic leads the thought, like a Sibyl compelled to prophesy, to the conclusions finally to be drawn from the premise, concerning both personal and communal life.

Dostoevsky does not define the object of all faith.[1] He contents himself with the description of two possibilities: man, whom he regards as free in the metaphysical sense, must give reality to this freedom (which is perhaps the only genuine freedom that he possesses) in the final decision between them. What is at issue here is not a mere intellectual preference for one of two hypotheses, but an acknowledgment and a decision arrived at by the heart.

"Euclidean" reasoning is concerned only with form: the comprehension of essence is a property of love alone. Only love can say "Thou art", and thus affirm the existence of the beloved. Only love effects a real connection between him who understands and the object of understanding; whereas, if love is extinguished, the spirit stands aloof, shut up in a sepulchral vault of mirrors.

The aporia of the human reason: that, on the one hand, empiric and divine reality seem to be mutually exclusive, whereas, on the other hand, the world without God loses not only its meaning, but also its reality—this aporia is resolved by the acknowledgment, which the heart can make at any time, of the value of Faith. The

---

[1] Dostoevsky does not admit a philosophy without premise. His very refined dialectic is based on a fundamental premise given by the first and determining decision taken by man. (*Note by the translator.*)

FREEDOM AND THE TRAGIC LIFE

first fruit of such an acknowledgment is the perception of the divine principle in man. Yet where can a human personality be found in which God's countenance shines so brightly that all doubts of His victory over the powers of death and darkness disappear? "Greater is He that is in you," says the Apostle, "than he that is in the world" (*First Epistle General of John* iv, 4). Where, then, is he the sight of whom would convince us of the truth of this saying? The highest truth that an acknowledgment by the heart can reveal is Jesus Christ. The peculiar quality of Dostoevsky's apologetic lies in its characteristic urge, not to found the love of Christ on belief in God, but to arrive through Christ at the certainty of God's existence. Which is the dream—God, or the world that denies Him? The hidden transcendent reality of God is attested by the directly perceived earthly reality of Christ. None cometh to the Father save through the Son. *Ecce Homo*. But if man, in his fulfilment, is as Christ is—then, too, the world, in all its sorry plight, is God's world, and no mere "Devil's farce".

Gazing down the furthest vistas of the two ways between which man has to make his final choice, and exploring in thought the most recondite laws of true and illusory being, Dostoevsky, quite unbeknown to himself, crosses the threshold of natural awareness of God. He gives expression to profound insights into the mystical life of the Church and the Communion of Saints (*communio sanctorum*), into the wonderful reality of the oneness of the human race in Christ, and into the essence of Evil and of holiness. To him the truths of revelation appear to carry in so high a degree their obviousness that they need only to be pointed out in order to exercise upon all men of goodwill their direct power of conviction. The ecclesiastical foundations of Faith become, like Plato's Orphic-Pythagorean corpus of dogma, the object of intuitively creative interpretation; and intuition, reinforced by dialectic, develops into an almost visionary contemplation of the transcendent. Moreover, just as for Plato the fortuitous manner in which occasions arise for the contemplation of one problem or another, and the apparent unconcern for the constructive homogeneity of the whole, in no way interfere with the unity of the total system, so for Dostoevsky the soul's flinchings as it penetrates the transcendent mystery, and the pangs of a slow spiritual parturition, imply no incoherence or fragmentariness in the insights thus achieved: on the contrary, these insights seem spontaneously to unite into a complete doctrinal system.

With astonishing logical exactitude Dostoevsky's marshalled thoughts deploy themselves throughout the series of his great works—from *Crime and Punishment* to *The Brothers Karamazov*. These poetically disconnected epics form, in truth—when considered in terms of the movement of living thought within them— the links of a dialectic chain, of theses and antitheses, the ladder of one continual ascent of the self-perceiving idea.

This is why, as a thinker, Dostoevsky can also be so misleading: the dialectical impetus of a spirit achieving awareness of itself is falsely interpreted, by some critics, as the expression of a radical scepticism and despair. They see in it the unintentional confession of "another soul" housed within this Centaur—for as such they see him. They regard him as a monstrous mixture of turbulent jail-bird and hypocritical Pharisee; and they unwearyingly endeavour, by listing contradictory statements that he has put into the mouths of his seekers and deniers of God, to convict him of disbelief in that which he solemnly proclaims as his final judgment. This theory is tenable on grounds neither of biography nor of psychology (to Dostoevsky, with his passionate nature, irony of any sort is almost as foreign as it is to Dante), nor yet of logic; and it can be equally well refuted by a study either of the context of the particular passages in which the negative attitude is expressed, or of the great organic unity of Dostoevsky's work as a whole. Indeed, all parts of his "doctrine" have such an inwardly fundamental and living relationship—his ethics, psychology, metaphysics, anthropology, sociology and eschatology so utterly determine and complement each other—that the deeper we penetrate into the nature of the connection between them, the more certainly must we come to realize that for Dostoevsky the creation of literary form was only a medium for the polymorphous development of a synthetic idea of the universe, which from the outset he had carried within him as a comprehensive vision and a morphological principle of his spiritual growth.

He himself speaks to us, in the person of Myshkin, of "these gleams and flashes of the highest sensation of life and self-consciousness in the ecstatic condition that heralds attacks of epilepsy, when the sense of life, the consciousness of self were multiplied ten times: mind and heart were flooded with extraordinary light, all his uneasiness, all his doubts, all his anxieties were relieved at once; they were all merged in a lofty calm, full of serene harmonious joy and hope, sustained by the revelation of the highest understanding of the first cause of things."[1] This comprehensive, total vision was an inward spiritual discernment of things in God; it was no mere contemplation of phantoms. Like every true

---

[1] Translation from the Russian original by Constance Garnett.

mystical experience, it was for the mystic himself, on the one hand, more certain than the world perceptible by the senses; yet, to his fellow-men, on the other hand, it was incommunicable, incapable of definition in the language of intellectual concepts, incomprehensible by the reason. That is why Myshkin, when describing his conversation with an atheist, states that the latter's reflections seemed to him, irrespectively of their degree of rational persuasiveness, simply incommensurable with the articles of Faith. The atheist continually "seemed not to be talking about the main point, the whole time. There seemed to be something else here . . ." he continues, "there will always be something else . . . something that atheists will for ever slur over; they will never be coming to *the* point".

Even today Dostoevsky's philosophy of life has not yet been revealed in its complete continuity. His contemporaries recognized and praised him primarily as a psychologist. They emphasized two characteristics of his "cruel talent"; and thereby determined, for a long time to come, the attitude adopted towards him, if not by the main body of responsive readers, at least by the appointed arbiters of literature. The first of these two characteristics is a noble, though morbid, preoccupation with the sufferings and mortifications of humiliated personalities, and the second is an exceptional trenchancy in the analysis of spiritual experience. His metaphysical defence of the personality was—luckily for his success!—for a long time not noticed.

Dostoevsky himself complains of this preconceived and one-sided assessment, which completely ignores the objective truth of his deepest and "most real" discoveries. He is not content with giving artistic and symbolic expression to the wealth of intuitions in his soul. He seeks—as Dante does in "The Banquet" and in the treatise *De Monarchia*—after forms that are directly didactic. In his *Journal of an Author* he describes—within a framework of exoteric comments dealing more or less immediately with current events—some aspects of his sole and unchanging "doctrine", whose inner form and true essence he can comprehend in its fullness and purity only when it is mirrored in myth: like all artists, whose task it is, in the words of Plato, to create myths (μύθους) and not doctrines (λόγους).

Since the beginning of this century attempts have been made to fathom Dostoevsky's symbols, and also his particular *placita* and *paradoxa*. His ideas have served, however, chiefly as a point of departure for various independent ideologies, tinged with mysticism, that readily sprang up from the rich soil of his titanic problematology. In our modern and more sober times, investigation is directed almost exclusively towards matters of fact and problems of form; that is to say, on the one hand towards biography, and on the other hand towards the technique of narration, towards questions of style, subject, artistic methods and literary-historical derivations. The investigation of Dostoevsky's religious philosophy remains as a serious task for the future.

The purpose of this sketch is to shed light on some connections—hitherto, in our opinion, not sufficiently explained—between the various well-known theses of a man whose conception of the Church's doctrine is entirely peculiar to himself. We seek to play the modest role of an interpreter, but of one who has his own peculiar interpretation. The reader must not be misled by the occasionally subjective tone of this exposé; the author has no wish to obtrude his own personal opinions. Without subscribing to every article of Dostoevsky's creed, he chooses to adopt the general attitude of an earnest pupil who strives—partly by his own arguments, what though they be clumsy—to convince others of the truth of his master's teachings. He wishes to communicate, with the bluntness of a zealot, his conception of, and his conclusions from, all that he himself has been offered and has absorbed. His loyalty to what he has been taught expresses itself in a sort of creative easiness in its rendering. He is convinced of his orthodoxy; for, without adhering to the letter of his text, he possesses—so it seems to him—an infallible criterion of this orthodoxy: the accord between what Dostoevsky had to teach and the living artistic imagery in which he clothed it.

Chapter I

DAEMONOLOGY

I

LUCIFER and Ahriman—the archetype of isolation and the archetype of destruction—the spirit of the light which may be darkness (*St. Luke* xi, 35) and the spirit of the black abyss: these are the two powers that fight against God in the world; or, rather, they are the two different masks of a single power that works in "the sons of rebellion"—the power whose name is Satan.

Since, however, hypostatic unity is the characteristic of absolute Being, whereas Evil, in its ontological nullity, simultaneously denies and imitates true Being (otherwise it would have not even the appearance of a positive content, without which its existence would be impossible), it follows that both these two patterns of an entity that is no true entity appear in separation and mutual negation. Neither of them, however, can achieve an original self-determination each on its own behalf, and both are compelled to seek their substance— as they find to their horror—each in its counterpart, reproducing each in itself the other's abysmal depths, like two empty mirrors confronting one another.

We do not mention these two Daemons in order to persuade our enlightened contemporaries of the spectral presence of the power of Evil in our scientifically investigated and well-swept civilization: our purpose is merely to show them. Their characters are so distinct, the ideas they embody are so clearly stamped upon their outward shapes, that we consider it highly instructive to draw the contrast and comparison between these two commanders of that citadel which—in the words of St. Augustine—is erected on earth by "the love of self that ends in hatred of God", and thus to recognize the forces that brought about the Fall of man and that feed his enmity towards God. The immediate purpose of this contrast is to clarify and deepen the sense of the fundamental difference that Dostoevsky sees between two types of human being and between two types of society— the God-proclaiming and the God-opposing—and thus to put in its true light his religiously ideal world of the future.

Dostoevsky does not call the two Daemons by different names; but never was an artist more sharply and deeply discerning in his examination of the peculiar properties of each, and of the different roads they take to the master of the human soul. When, in *Crime and Punishment*, Raskolnikov and Svidrigailov try to gaze into each other's natures, and the former—full of loathing at the bottom of his soul—has to agree with his counterpart when the latter declares that the fatal bond between them is not fortuitous, that they have an essential affinity, and resemble enemy twins—then it is Lucifer that dwells in one of them, and Ahriman who holds the other prisoner; and it is these two powers that survey, each within the other, the yawning black depths that are in both. For Dostoevsky, the two Daemons are two manifestations of *one* substance; which is not, however, of necessity completely represented by this duality, but, on the contrary, contains in its Satanic depths a third, and female, figure, the "Beauty of Sodom" which Dostoevsky, that explorer of Hell, contrasts with the Beauty of Our Lady.

The devil within Ivan Karamazov, it may be added—although, as the spirit of insipidity and triviality, it is a small but typical representative of the Legion of Ahriman—nevertheless develops the thoroughly Luciferian thesis (which it proclaims as its own, in the words: "Stupid fellows, they didn't ask *my* advice") when it asserts: "As soon as men have, all of them, denied God, man will be lifted up with a spirit of divine, Titanic pride, and the man-God will appear."[1]

But what need has Ahriman of this lifting-up of man? "Everyone will know," the Devil goes on, "that he is utterly mortal, without resurrection, that it's useless to repine at life's being a moment . . . and he will love his brother without need of reward."[1] The attitude is one of Luciferian loftiness, but the emphasis on the fact that man is mortal—utterly mortal, without resurrection—conveys to us Ahriman's whole nature: his elementary desire, and his quite fixed resolve, to rot and rend man's outer shell in order to deliver his inmost will to corruption, in order to destroy in man the image and likeness of God, in order to kill man's spirit.

"Men will unite," declares the Devil, "to take from life all that it can give, for nothing else but for joy and happiness in the present world." This union in the Devil's name, and the consequent "everything is permitted"—these constitute Ahriman's entire programme: he sets out by sensual enticements to abduct the spirit into the chaos of matter not yet awakened into Being; so that the light may be "engulfed in the

---

[1]Translation from the Russian original by Constance Garnett.

darkness", and there smothered and extinguished; so that man's inner character, which in its wholeness partakes of true Being, may fall to pieces in sensuality and vice, and that nothing may be left of the "man-God" but "a heap of rotting remains".

Is such an extinction and destruction of the spirit possible? The Revelation of St. John speaks mysteriously of a "second death".

2

To repeat what has already been said: if we posit, on the one hand, Lucifer shining in phosphorescent radiance —the ring-leader and standard-bearer of eternal revolt— the original inciter of man's proud longing for a godlike existence—the "sorrowful Daemon" who shone before Lermontov in "Beauty of enchanting sweetness", after his apparition had already enchanted Byron—the "mighty, dread and wise spirit", as Dostoevsky's Grand Inquisitor describes him; and if we posit, on the other hand, the all-disrupting, all-defiling and malignant Ahriman, the spectre of Evil in all the blackness of his shamelessly displayed vacuity and final nullity; if we posit these two as different countenances of one power, we shall be regarded by many as victims of a sinister, fanatical and misanthropic delusion.

Many people clearly see that the whole of our hybrid human civilization has come into being with the powerful and all-permeating participation and aid of Lucifer; that not only our destructive, but also our productive energies are, to a great extent, *his* energies; that it is he who makes us appear so fine to ourselves in the audacity of our haughty entrance on the scene, in our inflexible self-assertion, in the daring of our struggles for power and fame; and that, what though he also leads us to disaster, it is he again who vouchsafes us a proud self-satisfaction in the heroism of suffering. We are here concerned, however, not with the romantic charms of Daemonism, but with something infinitely more important and more real: with the evaluation of the primitive forces and basic motives of human nature. The more perspicacious go still further: they see and well know that the very conditions of our consciousness (isolated as it is, and hopelessly caught and confined as it appears to be in the doctrines of Kant), and even the very structure of our bodies (the Pentagram, the "organized egoism", as V. Solovyev calls it)—that these are manifestations of the Luciferian principle of spiritual self-preoccupation that is inherent in the children of Adam. And this is the reason why they do not dare to trace the deepest roots of our isolated and individual existence to the world of "the Evil One".

Yet we cannot ignore the fact that the denial of the evil innate in man's nature impoverishes and blunts our conception of man's true mission, of his tragic greatness and metaphysical dignity. Thus humanism, for example, knows no higher ideal than the general harmonious development of the natural resources of the personality, which is seen as an historically conditioned phenomenon within our sphere of civilization. This is the attitude of anthropological optimism which shrinks from the acceptance of "Original Sin"—that is to say, of the original self-determination exercised by man's will on the occasion of the Fall from God, together with all the consequences of this metaphysical event—and prefers to regard man as a product of a progressive evolution; without observing that man is degraded rather than ennobled by this notion—rather invited to renounce his highest privileges than encouraged to prevail over himself.

What, then, is the relationship between these two Daemons in their joint effect upon mankind?

Lucifer is an all-confining, Ahriman an all-disrupting power. The Lucifer in man is the principle of selfish aloofness, of proud independence, of wilful self-assertion and self-detachment from the Whole, of self-estrangement from the divine universal unity. Lucifer proclaims to men: "Ye shall be as gods," and he keeps his promise. The *single* Adam described in the Gospel as "the Son of God" is dispersed into a multiplicity of "would-be divine" personal and individual wills. Nevertheless, the divinity of mankind remains an accepted fact even in this dispersal—so much so that the personal consciousness contains not only the whole Creation, but also God as an idea. But this likeness of man to God is not real, but exists only in thought, confined in the inner world of the personality—confined so strictly that the personality feels imprisoned in its solitude and despairs of its own being.

This despair, then, is what Ahriman exploits, to induce man to say in his heart: "I am not." At this point the whispered messages of the two Daemons become different: Lucifer abuses the divine "I am" that dwells within man, by distorting its meaning, and thus also distorting that innermost human will (as in the case of Raskolnikov). Ahriman, the corrupter of the human will, reveals the vacuity of the "I am" itself where it lives in a will that is depraved and decaying (as in the case of Svidrigailov).

The influence of Lucifer can therefore be described as inversionary, and that of Ahriman as perversionary.

But now let us consider what is the essence of the human "I am", and how one may conceive of its depravation.

3

When the divine "I am" was bestowed upon man the son of God, who is created that he may lovingly recognize and freely desire his Sonship, and thus become truly "born" of God (as it is written: "Ye must be born on high")—then, in this fatherly sacrifice made by God, occurred the creation of man through God and in God's image.

Lucifer tempts men to cease from construing this "I am", this fatherly gift, in a manner befitting a son ("I and the Father are one"), and, instead, to exploit the gift in the manner of a rebellious creature, and to proclaim: "I exist wholly in myself, for myself, and apart from everything else.[1] I suffice unto myself, and all that is not my Ego I repudiate and do not recognize. I see it not, I hear it not, I remember it not, I know it not. Or, alternatively, I contain it within myself: behold, I devour it, in order to bring it forth anew from within myself as a manifestation and utterance of my Ego."

Thus Lucifer greedily seizes the divine "I am" and sucks it, as it were, into himself; but he cannot make it real. And man is left with that noble discontent that

---

[1] Directly hence results the formulation of the anarchist M. Bakunin: "God exists—then man is a slave. If man is free—then God does not exist." A subtler variant on this formulation is to be found in the early works of Rudolf Steiner, in a passage where he asserts that belief in a transcendent Godhead is incompatible with human freedom. But both pure transcendentism and pure immanentism serve alike, in their narrow exclusiveness, to pre-suppose and confirm man's Luciferian Fall from God. The one fully and completely acceptable theistic conception is that of Christianity, which does justice to both theories: it accomplishes that freeing of man which is foretold by the principle of the Covenant in the Old Testament, and also promises man, in his Sonship of God, victory over his creaturehood (the θέωσις of the Early Fathers).

distinguishes him from other creatures; he is bereft of his true being. He knows all too well that he *is*, but at the same time he knows that he will never be able worthily to utter his "I am". Therefore he is ashamed of his existence, which is *only* "an existence" (and herein he gives an indication of his spiritual nobility); or he dimly feels a sense of guilt in it because of his separate origin (*cf.* Anaximander).

Man's longing for true being presents itself to him in the guise of a "craving for immortality"; and according to Dostoevsky, belief in immortality is the origin of all man's creative and moral forces. But Lucifer has succeeded in shutting man up in his selfhood, and has deprived him of the possibility of direct contact with other worlds; so that now he is compelled to rely upon his own natural powers of reason, and comes to regard his "craving for immortality" (by which he means his longing for true being) as an empty and illusory claim.

For the truth is that Lucifer, by cutting man off from all that is real, has brought him to a point at which every reflection or echo of reality seems to him, who has now become "like God", to be his own creation, a product of his self-awareness. Lucifer has said to man: "Thou art he who can say, like God, 'I am'. Therefore thou art entitled to rule over the universe, to have it in thy power and, like God, to contain it within thyself." But when man asked, like Archimedes, for a foot's breadth of firm ground on which he could station and support himself in order to apply the lever of his divine omnipotence—why, then, the seducer vanished, and man was left suspended in the void of that world within himself, that world created by his thoughts.

Thus from the beginning of man's history on earth Lucifer confronts man as his seducer and tempter. In order to triumph over this ordeal, man must himself find his other one to serve as his fulcrum. By the act of love, and of the faith that love contains and supports, he must win his "Thou art". Plato teaches that, as man ascends the stairway of love, at each new step he learns to recognize in the beloved an even greater participation in true Being; and thereby he himself grows in Being, in which he shares through the beloved, until finally, in his longing for absolute Being, which he seeks in the "Thou", he recognizes, by an ineffable incandescence within his heart, the One Beloved who in Himself contains, confirms and saves all other loves. Through Him man receives the consecration of the true Sonship of God.

But if man cannot by the act of his love win that beloved to whom he could cry out, with all his will and cognition, "Thou art"; and if the little lamp of his psyche, whose flame is his divine "I am", receives no oil supplied by another, then Ahriman draws near to him and asks him: "Wilt thou not now take thy heady yet bitter cup, on whose rim are written the dead words 'I am', and drink it to the lees? For already thou seest the bottom of the cup; and thou seest in the bottom of the cup: Not-being. Acknowledge that 'I am' is exhausted and at an end, because thou hast not found any to whom thou couldst in truth say 'Thou art'; because thou hast persuaded thyself that there is no God. Therefore canst thou thyself no longer be."

And the sign of man's personal power of endeavour, his five-pointed star, his Pentagram, which with its middle ray points towards Heaven (*os sublime fert*), the symbol of his motive force and active will—that which, in so far as it is truly active, must of necessity strive towards supremacy over self—the Pentagram turns upside down and plunges into the gaping void of Ahriman.

Thus Ahriman follows Lucifer: Faust's path is continually dogged by Mephisto, the instigator to evil deeds and also their perpetrator. Byron's noble Cain, who made friends with the Morning Star, slays his brother. Similar fates befall Dostoevsky's Luciferian characters: Raskolnikov murders the old woman; Stavrogin, after a series of crimes, commits suicide; Ivan Karamazov, without fully knowing what he is doing, makes evil use of Smerdyakov as an instrument of parricide.

4

Quite apart, however, from the fact that Lucifer's influence upon the human soul does not at all imply the soul's immediate destruction, but only a fearful test of its capacity to survive, this influence is, at the outset, a vast spiritual stimulus. It most powerfully heightens and intensifies all man's existential and creative energies. The sense of the "I am", gathering in the innermost depths of the personality as if at a point of combustion, expresses itself in a dialectical unfolding of all the spiritual riches and worlds slumbering within the mysterious "Am". The Luciferian force impels man, like the Goethean hero who calls himself a "superman" and in Heaven is named "the thrall of God", to strive by his own efforts "continually towards the supreme existence".

And Goethe is in the right when he announces that only the merit of its constant striving is what enables the soul to find redemption; and that if the soul be entered by love from on high, it will be saved the sooner.

The dark power can gain dominion over the soul only at moments of stagnation. Stagnation is disastrous: whether it is born, as it was for Faust, of self-complacency—as the sudden petrifaction of a pride sunk in self-admiration; or whether it consists in man's complete surrender to some passion in which Ahriman, ever on the watch, has ensnared him—the passion, for example, of easily provoked envy, such as afflicted Byron's *Cain*; in either case, it is but short-lived, and Ahriman is certain of his prey.

It follows, therefore, that the operation of Luciferian forces in man—a necessary consequence of that spiritual event, the defection from God which the Church calls the Fall of Man—is in this world a natural presupposition and basis of all our historical and, to this day, largely heathen civilization, and is, in truth, our civilization's Original Sin; for only in a few of its parts has this civilization received the sacrament of baptism, and only very rarely indeed does it reflect the splendour of Christ.

Lucifer's influence, although dangerous, is not ruinous —provided, at least, that man is continually active, unflaggingly subjugating all the forms of self-assertion that he has already mastered to new forms of a nobler existence. But it turns to deadly poison if the dynamic forces of the spirit are drowned in those dead waters of stagnation over which Ahriman spreads his black pinions.

Dostoevsky has depicted the realm of Ahriman as a stagnant decomposition of the Luciferian personality immured within itself—thus, in Svidrigailov's daydreams of eternity, it is a musty room with bolted doors and with spiders in its corners; and also as a slow process of putrefaction—as in the merry conversations of the cemetery's inmates in *Bobok*.

DAEMONOLOGY

Wherever the self-determination of the individual or of society has been reduced to stagnation, so that it finds its sustenance in itself and asserts itself as the supreme and self-sufficing principle—there, above the darkness of Ahriman, gleams like phosphorescent rottenness the reflection of Lucifer. It gleams (to revert again to *The Brothers Karamazov*, the novel that offers the clearest guidance to the understanding of these matters) even around that fettered captive of Ahriman, the old Karamazov, and is the secret cause of his grudge against God and his blasphemy.

5

Lucifer is "the Prince of this World", Ahriman is his executioner, his Satrap and—so he hopes—his royal successor. It is to Ahriman that dominion over the earth must pass, unless Lucifer is overthrown by Him who in the Revelation of St. John is called "the Morning Star", "Alpha and Omega", "the beginning and the end", "the first and the last", "the Lamb of God, who taketh away the sins of the world".

Throughout the New Testament, the words "earth" and "world" have meanings of their own, different from those of customary usage. "Earth" is associated with light, "World" with darkness. The "world" hates the incarnate Word, and those who have received the Word hate the "world". The "earth" is covered and shrouded, so to speak, by the "world", but does not itself belong to the world. Just as the sixth husband of the woman of Samaria is not her husband, so the Prince of this World is not the true spouse of Earth, but only her whore-master. His dominion over her is, in fact, the "World". The "World" is Earth's present condition, and Earth is only outwardly ruled by Lucifer—in her mode, but not in her substance. The seventh bridegroom—the Heavenly one, He that was promised and eagerly awaited, is He whom the woman recognizes in the stranger who says to her "give me to drink".

Lucifer's dominion over Earth does not penetrate to the depths of her mystic reality. He has severed all ties with reality, therefore he cannot touch it. His government of the world is purely ideal—like the "World" itself: it is lent reality by means of, and within, forms of thought and maxims of behaviour evolved by man. And whereas, according to Dostoevsky, salvation from Ahriman is only granted by Christ the Risen, Lucifer's realm of enchantment collapses merely on contact with the living Earth.

Lucifer is an idealist: his own realization, that he hates, is Ahriman. The true antagonists are Ahriman and Christ. Christ brings to creaturedom virginal wholeness and resurrection; Ahriman brings violation and putrefaction. This antagonism is symbolically expressed, in *The Brothers Karamazov*, in Alyosha's dream of the Lord's Supper—a dream that comes to Alyosha when he is dazed by the "smell of putrefaction" arising from Zosima's coffin and hears the monotonous voice of the monk reading the story of the marriage of Cana.

The decision between the two antagonists is given, in so far as it relates to historical earthly destinies, through man and in man. At present it is Lucifer who prevails in him and through him: Lucifer whose sway over our civilization is today apparent. The will of civilization is to subjugate nature by force; the will of nature is to devour civilization. Civilization, says Dostoevsky, in *A Raw Youth*, is a "state of orphanage", a "deep mourning for the setting sun". Civilization has reached its end—or its turning-point? All that it can do now is to escape by means of its own impetus: it must hasten and flee, ceaselessly flee, like a hunted animal. The "Prince of this World" hunts it with the pack of Ahriman. How much longer can it continue to flee?

The way of Lucifer—that is to say, the way of the history of civilization—ends at a bifurcation; and here Lucifer abandons the wayfarers, who henceforth must choose between the narrow path of Christ and the broad road of Ahriman. But at this stage of the journey only few will be able to take a free decision. Only those who have preserved their spiritual countenance will find in themselves the power to turn from the multitude and enter the citadel of God—like the Parable's labourers in the vineyard who began their work in the last hour of the day. The rest must charge, like a crazy herd, into that other citadel—the citadel of Legion.

Legion, like Lucifer and Ahriman, is not actually used as a symbol in Dostoevsky's works, but is unequivocally indicated. As an epigraph to *The Possessed* Dostoevsky sets the Biblical tale of the devils who dwelt in the mountain tombs of the country of the Gadarenes, and, after being cast out of the man whom they had possessed, entered into a herd of swine. Before Christ heals the possessed man, he asks him: "What is thy name?" And the man answers, speaking both in the singular and in the plural: "My name is Legion: for we are many."

Legion (*cf.* pp. 68-69 *et seq.*, and p. 140) is that already mentioned union between men of which Ivan Karamazov's devil says: "Men will unite to take from life all that it can give, but only for joy and happiness in the present world." This age of Legion will dawn as soon as the decomposition of the spiritual personality is complete.

The contemporary situation of a personality that has been rendered impotent through the weakening of its higher spiritual self-awareness, and loses itself in pitiable efforts to maintain its debased dignity and independence within a society that is as bad—because as loveless and irreligious—as itself, is analysed in Dostoevsky's *The Man from Underground*. Cravenly and spitefully such a personality withdraws into its little world, hidden from all men, and there maliciously hoards up its grievances, and takes its revenge upon society by crawling, like a crushed snake, out of its Ahrimanian hole and biting the first comer.

The "Underground Hero", although repulsive in his manner of life, is capable of clear-sighted and lofty meditation. And since Dostoevsky recognizes even in such a character the shrine of human dignity, and in the name of this takes his side against society, the author has no objection to uttering through the character's mouth the religious truth concerning society in its elementary form: the truth that relations between the personality and society must be founded on mutual love; that the personality must voluntarily place itself at the service of the good of all, and society must dedicate itself to the protection of the personality.

From this premise Dostoevsky develops a devastating criticism of present-day social relations, which he believes to be fundamentally unjust. No external means, however, are effective enough to remove the deeply rooted evil. By the law of this world the personality is condemned to lingering and wasting sickness: because it has shut itself up in itself, because it seeks to "preserve its soul". In its claims to an autonomous self-assertion, it no longer itself knows exactly what it is asserting. It strives to assert itself in its accidental attributes. These attributes, however, are such as incur either the judicial sentence of Fate: "This, and this, will turn to dust in the grave", or the sentence of the spirit of history, "This, and this, will be taken from the individual in the name of the preservation of species".

Everything, on the other hand, that the personality might have chosen to consecrate to God would have been preserved unto itself, would in that case have developed itself to greater abundance, and would thus itself have become enriched. But the personality was miserly, greedy and mistrustful: it ceased to trust in God and to believe in Him, and, as an immediate consequence, it lost its faith in itself as a true being.

He who loves knows the beloved, and has no doubt of the beloved's being; but the man who has slackened in his love has been afraid of wasting the soul's fire in the wilderness of the world, and has therefore directed his entire love towards himself. If it is correct that, as Nietzsche says, man has up to this moment yielded his best treasure to God, he now seeks to take back all his gifts; but in his hands these prove to be a pile of ashes left over from his own burnt sacrifice. Then man comes to realize that, like the Prodigal Son, he has become a beggar, because he receives no more gifts from God; and he sees that he has no longer a face, because the bright Heavenly face has been blotted out, and with it also the image of God in his soul. Love is the interaction in reality of the life of reality.

If love is extinguished, then also is extinguished the sense of the reality of the once loved Being. Once the personality has lost its love towards God, it begins to love itself, its desires are turned inward upon itself, and it destroys itself. It forgets and betrays its own divine element, by striving only after the human—which melts beneath its hands and flees like a shadow.

The soul that has lost its treasure of love and faith may be likened in its attitude towards the personality which has found its self-determination in God, which nourishes its abundance for God's sake and thrives in God's name, unto a little, shrivelled tree that seeks to pour contumely upon a live, healthy tree for wasting its strength upon its young shoots.

"But I grow towards the sun," says the healthy tree.

"There is no sun," says the little, shrivelled tree. "Neither I nor you can see it."

"But I feel the sun, it's so lovely to open out to its warmth and, as it were, to touch it with ever new and sprouting buds."

"I, too, feel the warmth," answers the little, shrivelled tree. "It is a condition that repeats itself in us regularly: a condition known as Spring. But I am not so credulous as you are, and I reserve all my sap for my own inner sustenance."

So the little, shrivelled tree continues in the delusion that it is inwardly self-sufficient, until the gardener comes and cuts it down.

7

The final phase of the personality's struggle for existence occurs when the personality proves its impotence in face of the principle of species. Infallible observation of the rule *divide et impera* has given the Prince of this World his greatest possible power over men. Throughout all the centuries of modern history he has divided men from one another by teaching the personality to regard itself as its own autonomous essence ("Antichrist will found his cause on anarchy," says Dostoevsky), and to enclose itself within itself. The rebellious pride of Adam has been pounded into an atomically fine dust of self-love, pretensions and grievances. Between the impenetrable components of this dust there can be no voluntary alliance, unless on the grounds of a mechanical co-operation for selfish ends. The old links of organic cohesion have been slackened by the internal disruption. All forms of utilitarian community of interests, amongst members of the same species to preserve this species, are regarded as ways and means to the salvation of whatever particular individual.

A time is coming that will be under the sign, not merely of a close social integration, but also of new forms of collective consciousness. Then mankind approaches, as we have already said, a parting of ways, which lead to the two citadels of which St. Augustine wrote: "Two citadels were built by two kinds of love: love of self, that ends in contempt of God, raised unto itself the Earthly Citadel; and love of God, that ends in contempt of self, raised the Heavenly Citadel." And henceforth no man will ever be able to suppose that he is outside one or other of these citadels, and no man will be able to preserve his solitude upon earth. Not only the outward, but also the inward possessions of man will be tied, by the bond of the responsibility of all men for all men, to the inner destiny of man's entire environment. All life will become one whole, and each entity a part of the whole entity. The host of Antichrist will appear to have an even closer inward unity than that of the host of Christ, but it will only appear to do so. The principles of unification in each of these two communities, hosts or citadels, will be utterly opposed.

The Earthly Citadel (in St. Augustine's sense), the bulwark of resistance to, and hatred of, God, will have reached its completion at the moment when personality is finally submerged in totality. Yet the sign of this city, the sign of Antichrist, will be set only upon him who proves himself incapable of preserving his personality—and not, it goes without saying, of preserving it in vain pretensions or in the superficial self-will of the outer man, but as his inflexible power of free self-determination before God and man, as his inner being and the holy aspirations and desires of his heart. Man's most eager endeavour at the present time must be, therefore, to sanctify freedom, to experience it with dignity and reverence, to recognize it within himself and relinquish it to none—unless in voluntary obedience to that which in his innermost heart he has acknowledged as the supreme law.

In these times faith in God must be linked with a deep and integral experience of a living faith in the true existence of an inextinguishable and deeply hidden Ego in man. This experience, which takes the form of belief in the immortality of the soul, is also a certain consequence and corollary of faith in God. The poetry of Byron is seen by Dostoevsky as man's competitive emulation of God, and as a great and holy manifestation of the European spirit—for the very reason that this contest with God arises from the assertion of the essentially immortal and divine human personality. If faith in God begins to waver, the sense of the inner personality is lost; and this loss leads, in turn, to an easily vulnerable self-love and conceit, to the spiritual condition of "The Man from Underground", to despondency and to the fatal self-betrayal of suicide.

The more pride puts forth its Hydra's heads, the more

deeply is its ephemeral subject, the "proud man" (as Dostoevsky describes the Luciferian type) humiliated in his own eyes, until he sees himself as a chance conglomeration of cells. Thus today the question of faith is naturally no longer, as in olden times, "Do you believe in God?", but first of all, "Do you believe in your Ego, that it truly exists, that it transcends your ephemerality and darkness and is greater than you in your impotence and littleness?" For modern science knows nothing of the real being of an Ego, which has become an object of pure belief, as much so as the being of God.

8

The link between men and a unity achieved by de-personalization must necessarily bring about a development of the collective centres of consciousness, and create, as it were, a joint collective brain, which will immediately surround itself with a complicated and delicate nervous system. This organism will inevitably assume the shape of a social animal distinguished by an immense strength and by an extreme purposefulness in all the movements of a body adapted to strict subordination and centralization, a body that is essentially mechanical, yet, in a sense, possessed of a soul.

This will be the evolution of a part, and indeed the numerically greater part, of humanity into the Great Beast of which, according to the prophecy in the Revelation, it will be said: "Who is like unto this Beast?" This evolution will be at the same time the apotheosis of organization; for the Beast will be society organized to the utmost. The denial of the Church as the Kingdom of Heaven upon earth must necessarily lead to a deification of the "Leviathan" described by Hobbes. A tendency towards this can be detected in Hegel's doctrine of the State, and still more clearly in the Marxian ideal of the Dictatorship of the Proletariat. Shortly before his death, Dostoevsky wrote in his diary: "Until now we have not seen any absolute, or even a more or less complete, State. They are all mere embryos." The multiplicity of de-personalized individuals, bound by no universal oneness in love, is, in fact, Legion, of whom we have already spoken.

The problem of Legion, which for us is so insistent, is one of the impenetrable mysteries of Evil. Man's spiritual privilege, which is also a symbol of his divine nature, is that he can apprehend only true Being, and not its distorted reflection in the realm of Evil. As a son of the Word he can apprehend the meaning only of that which has a part in the Word. How separation can become a principle of union, how hatred may fuse together the mutually hating elements—these things are, in their nature, fortunately beyond our understanding. Yet the presence of daemonic Legion, who speaks at once as "I" and as "we" is a phenomenon that actually confronts us.

The sort of co-operation displayed by Legion is to some extent conceivable only if one assumes that it represents a mechanically organized accumulation of atoms produced by an evil power that has fallen to dust; and that this power must have been so evil that its inherent inner discord has lost its own unity and has broken up into a multiplicity, which thereupon unwillingly exploits a sort of natural cohesion in order to generate a mechanical life in its disparate parts and invest the whole, like a galvanized corpse, with the appearance of life. But the particles that make up this apparent whole are not live monads, but dead souls, the dust-storm of Hell.

Thus it is that even human society, as soon as it takes devilish Legion as its model, must begin to weaken the ontological sense of the personality and to deprive personality of its spiritual countenance. Its drastic dismemberment and specialization must slowly and inevitably exaggerate each individual's purely functional energies, and methodically stifle to death his spiritual self-awareness.

The oecumenical oneness of all in Christ, on the other hand, is a union in which the uniting personalities achieve a complete development and a clear outlining of their peculiar and original entities—of their integral creative freedom. In each of them the Word has found its embodiment. It dwells in all, and from each it is heard in a different and especial fashion. Yet the Word in the utterance of each is echoed in all; and all are the one free unity, for all are the One Word.

Firm confidence in the realization of this Christian universal oneness upon earth is a sacred possession of the Russian people: this is what, in Dostoevsky's view, makes it a "God-bearing people". The solemn proclamation and complete development of this idea—an idea that inspired Dostoevsky in all his works—are to be found in his last novel, to which we shall now turn.

Chapter II

HAGIOLOGY

I

IN *The Brothers Karamazov* Russia is portrayed in the persons of the three brothers, of whom the youngest is marked out by his quiet humility—like a character in a fairy-tale—as the elect of Fate.

True-hearted Dimitri, the eldest son of Feodor Karamazov—that hopeless slave of Ahriman—represents the nature of the people. He has a sense of brotherhood with the simple peasantry, he shares in its faith, its attitude towards life and its general temperament. Like the people, he has a deep feeling for the living mystery of Mother Earth (it is not by chance that his name is a derivation of "Demeter"), and he finds in loving contact with her the strength to praise life and its Creator in the midst of terrible agonies of the soul.

Despite all this, Dimitri is always in danger of becoming completely a prey to Ahriman. Even the high nobility of spirit that he has inherited from his mother cannot restrain him from shameful and outrageous acts of unruly passion. Even his moments of great and holy inspiration bring him to no rebirth. With agonizing certainty Dimitri recognizes both the "Cherub" in himself, the Cherub that "stands before God", and also the "worm" which, as Schiller says, "is yielded up to lust". Schiller's *Hymn to Joy*, and the lines describing the sorrow of Ceres at the sight of man's degradation (in "The Eleusinian Festival") are for Dimitri like a prayer that he is never weary of repeating. Dimitri's childishly naïve and trustful, chaotically uncontrolled, indeed sometimes bestially unbridled, nature needs to find its purification in suffering. He is a sacrifice of atonement for all the wild but anciently established Russia of old, corrupt morals and, at the same time, of age-long and sound tradition, through whose Ahrimanian night gently shines the Holy Russia, like a brightly lit church seen from afar. From Lucifer, on the other hand, Dimitri—thanks to his loyalty to Earth, who protects man against a delusive, presumptuous and self-bound introversion—he is more free than almost anybody else in the world; for to the Ahriman within him he never says "Yea" or "Amen", but lives in perpetual remorse and sorrow of heart for his captivity and baseness, in perpetual penitence for his sinfulness.

The second brother, the well-educated Ivan, the son of that glorious martyr, Feodor Karamazov's second wife, represents the Russia that is estranged from the people and misleads the people: the Russia of Lucifer. His atheism is so perplexedly intellectual that it contains the possibility of a revulsion—in abstract thought, at least—into its opposite. His vassalage to Lucifer is almost conscious. This is why the darkness of Ahriman thickens around his Luciferian light, and brings forth from itself, as its other Ego, not only the spectre of the "trencher-friend-Devil", but also the reality of the servant Smerdyakov, his illegitimate brother, who hates Russia because he is a bastard and the son of a harlot. Ivan, grown insane with horror, repulsion and despair, clearly feels how Ahriman is using this henchman—who despises Ivan, is Ivan's image, and destroys Ivan by guessing his most secret will and ruthlessly carrying it out—to ensnare him in an inescapable and hellish noose. Ivan recognizes himself as the other face of the parricide, just as Smerdyakov recognizes Ivan. Is not Lucifer himself in the same fashion entangled, to his fearful torment, with his black double?

The youngest brother, Alyosha, takes entirely after his mother: "Though he lost his mother in his fourth year, he remembered her all his life—her face, her caresses, 'as though she stood before me'. He remembered one still summer evening, an open window, the slanting rays of the setting sun (that he recalled most vividly of all); in a corner of the room the holy image, before it a lighted lamp, and on her knees before the image his mother, sobbing hysterically with cries and moans, snatching him up in both arms, squeezing him till it hurt, and praying for him to the Mother of God, holding him out in both arms to the image as though to put him under the Mother's protection."[1]

The wrong done to his mother had a bitter and life-long effect upon Alyosha. But the feeling aroused in him was not directed against his father, but against the power that held his father captive—against Ahriman. It is from Ahriman that he flees—but not to Lucifer, as all modern Russia has done, and as Ivan did, but to seek refuge with the Orthodox "starzy".

2

From childhood onwards, Alyosha's distinguishing and peculiar blessing, which introduces him, so to

---

[1] Translation from the Russian original by Constance Garnett.

speak, into the nation's Holy of Holies, is the grace of an all-transcending, passionately burning love of Christ. "Perhaps the Russian people's only love is Jesus Christ," Dostoevsky writes in *The Journal of an Author*, "and it loves Christ's figure in its own way: that is to say, to the point of suffering." This is the light that shines before the youth on his path encompassed by the shades of Hell, and effects so wonderful a peace in him that he strides forward courageous and strong, nay, joyful and happy. He says himself that he can distinguish between good and evil only because he has before him the image of Christ. This longing for the Only One, for the whiteness that is purer than the purest snow, for the Sun of Resurrection shining from the earth's depths, grows within Alyosha, as within his people, out of a life plunged in darkness where Evil has already renounced all masks, out of a continual confrontation with the black spectre of Ahriman.

A characteristic yearning, born *de profundis*, for the countenance of Christ is, according to Dostoevsky, that which most deeply animates, saves and sanctifies the Russian nation; and it seems to him that the Russian soul has for centuries shed so many tears before this countenance, has devoted so much of its best energies to the profoundest experience of the Christian faith, has sacrificed so much of its spiritual being to win the pearl of great price, that it can truly no longer accomplish anything creative, unless it be something born of this Faith and returning as additional wealth to the Faith's treasury. And Dostoevsky abides by this opinion even when, gazing, as it were, into the future, he already begins to guess that even the greatest devotion cannot in the time of utmost trial be a safeguard against the temptations of a general defection. In *The Journal of an Author*, an entry made in 1873 relates—in reference to the coming revolution, which Dostoevsky clearly foresaw — an "extremely characteristic and highly symptomatic incident": how a peasant youth led astray by a friend ("perhaps by some village Nihilist, some home-made all-denier and thinker") had laid a wager that he would commit the most audacious act imaginable, and aimed a gun at a fragment of the Host which, at his comrade's bidding, he had stolen from the Mass. "He merely had to press the trigger, that was all." Then suddenly he saw before him the Cross, and on the Cross the Crucified, and swooned, with his gun in his hand. A few years later he crawled on his knees to a *starez* and begged "to be allowed to suffer".

This story affords Dostoevsky an occasion to subject the Russian revolt against God to a penetrating analysis, which leads him to the unexpected conclusion that it is just such "new men" who, "whether or not they do penance", will say "the last word", and that these will be the men "who will show us the new way and the new escape".

"That valiant hero, the people," Dostoevsky continues, "is awakened and stretching his limbs. Perhaps he will feel a desire to carouse, to kick over the traces; but at the last moment all that is false will leap from his heart and present itself before him with all its terrible strength of conviction, and he will come to himself and begin the work of God. Come what may, he will save himself, even if everything is already close to the brink of disaster; he will save himself and us, for light and salvation will begin to shine from below, from the lowliest strata of the people . . ." Unshakable is Dostoevsky's belief in the soul of the people as a treasure-house of the deepest Christian sentiment.

"The work of God" that the Russian people "will begin"—an initial step, that is to say, towards the metamorphosis and transfiguration of all life by this Christian sentiment—is no doubt synonymous with the birth of "the future independent Russian idea", of which Dostoevsky says here and elsewhere that "it is not yet born among us, but the earth is big with it, and is preparing to bring it forth with fearful pangs". However distant the future to which this expectation may apply, Alyosha's mission is obviously connected with it.

Alyosha, this "perhaps even active character, but an active character that is unformed, not yet brought to full definition", as the author remarks apologetically, with a secret smile, of the young hero of his unfinished novel; this "oddity" who yet perhaps carries within him "the nucleus of the whole", whereas "all other people of his time are swept away from this nucleus by some sudden gust of wind"—Alyosha, unbeknownst to himself, is one of the first-born of a third Russia, which is completely different from the second, or Luciferian, Russia. It is the new "Holy Russia", and this Holy Russia is the daughter. The mother has turned away from the world, has withdrawn to distant regions, to an ancestral hermitage, and has sent her beloved daughter into the world to renew the name and countenance of Christ in the memory of those who have gone astray, to scatter anew the Christian seed in the furrows of a changed era.

If this is so, it is worth our while—the more so since many critics have asserted that Alyosha, as a type and symbol, is altogether lacking not only life but any sort of content—to examine whether already on his first appearance, in his years of preparation (for we know nothing of his later life), Alyosha carries any seed of the religious action expected of him as an active character. It is, at any rate, historically indisputable that Dostoevsky's preaching is directly connected with a powerful upsurge of religious thought led by Vladimir Solovyev at its head.

3

What kind of a person is the monk Alyosha? An agreeable youth, still almost a boy, of a candid and cheerful nature, but already at an early age having to suffer for himself and for others, to suffer the sorrow of a heart that shares in wisdom. He is as fresh and modest as a young girl; so chaste that obscene talk and behaviour cause him intense pain and a horror that is, so to speak, metaphysical. He is religious, but without a touch of bigotry. Despite his novice's cowl, he is no fanatical observer of rites. Altogether he is little suited to a contemplative life, but he is kind and always at hand where advice and help are needed. He is clever, though without book-learning. He involuntarily exercises an attraction upon all hearts. He lays claim to nothing, he covets nothing for himself, and, as a truly free man, he is immune from the universal infirmity of his time—that of self-love—and is therefore at once invulnerable and incorruptible. A youth who never shrinks from making up his own mind how to act, or from appearing ridiculous in the eyes of men, he fears neither the tempting proximity, nor any disastrous upset, of the circumstances of daily life, nor yet the poisonous thoughts that put his deepest religious convictions to the test. He is hot-tempered, yet gentle; sympathetic, yet firm. Perhaps he is an "early lover of humanity", yet none the less gifted with the first elements of shrewd discernment, and certainly also with a quite uncommon

understanding of the human soul and its hidden passions;
a lover of humanity, however, who does not entitle us
to expect from him, even in his future and still quite
uncertain activities, anything more than a deep spiritual
response to, and a practical readiness to help, the human
beings of his environment—so remote is he from any
urge towards a businesslike or heroic participation in
the building of human relations.

In Dostoevsky's words, had Alyosha not believed in
God, he would have joined the Socialists. As it is,
however, he might be described as a philanthropist of
religious tendency, who is however by no means a
politician or revolutionary, or even an active reactionary.
(The fact that he is not this last is an annoyance to those
who mistrust him; for, were he but a reactionary,
everything would be much simpler.) He appears to be
by nature incapable of supporting by thought or action
any cause save those of liberty, equality and fraternity;
and these only in Christ, and not in Lucifer—a
reservation that to many people is synonymous with
"passive reaction".

Alyosha's behaviour makes him appear to be in
practice a disciple of the doctrine of "non-resistance";
but even as such he compromises himself—as when
Ivan tells him of some landowner who had a serf's child
hunted to death by dogs, and Alyosha exclaims, in words
entirely meaningless to bourgeois ears: "Shoot him!"
What can that sort of thing have to do with any programme of social reform? Besides, if we examine the
matter more closely, we find that Alyosha is, above all,
the communal man. Community is, first and foremost,
union of human beings; and around Alyosha occurs,
so to speak, a spontaneous union. His youth, which is
portrayed in the novel, ends in the foundation, under his

influence, of a life-long brotherhood of boys, and in the oath of eternal loyalty to the memory of Ilyusha and to all the goodness that this remembrance teaches: and what does it not teach, in the field of religion, of ethics, or of social life?

The symbol of this compact is all the more significant because Alyosha was by this time no longer a boy. Apart from all the trials to which his soul has been subjected by his brothers and by the bride whom destiny has chosen for him, it is primarily an inward experience that has made him spiritually a man and a sage: an experience that can be described only in the words "mystical consecration". For something extraordinary happened to him in the monastery after Zosima's death: after a brief but terrible Luciferian "revolt" in the depths of his soul, he was seized with a hitherto unguessed-at ecstasy, and "felt clearly and, as it were, tangibly that something firm and unshakable as that vault of heaven had entered his soul"[1]—that "he had fallen on the earth a weak boy, but he rose up a resolute champion, and he knew and felt it suddenly, at the very moment of his ecstasy".[1] This moment had occurred when "someone visited his soul"[1]; whereupon he, three days later, left the monastery in order, at Zosima's bidding, "to sojourn in the world".[1]

Thus begins Alyosha's activity in the world, which consists in bringing about an especial sort of connection between the people who surround him. This connection is not established for the pursuit of any particular aim, nor yet in the service of any clearly defined idea. It is the connection between men in the name of a personality that is close to all of them and profoundly holds all of them together: the personality of Ilyusha, who in his

---

[1]Translation from the Russian original by Constance Garnett.

life was at once child and hero, rebel and martyr, and now, after his transfiguration by death, is no longer child or hero, rebel or martyr, but *himself* in his entirety— himself as he will eventually, on the day of resurrection, return in his unique and inimitable personality to the former school-mates who persecuted and tormented him, but have now become his dearest friends and brothers in Christ.

It is important to comprehend the personal and real character of the Ilyusha brotherhood. The connection between its individual members is not such as to make each of them contribute to the community only something definable and consciously separate, something detached from the generality of his spiritual life, a mere part of his feelings, his intellectual interests or the impulses of his will. The connection resembles, rather, a ceremonial chalice passed around a table: a cup in which once upon a time—during the bitter yet richly consoling period of a shared childhood that was still almost unsullied by any guilt—the shared guilt and the shared forgiveness were mingled together; as if Ilyusha's entire life were for ever laid abundantly and accommodatingly over the life of each one of the participants in the ceremony, and each life had encountered each of the other lives in and through Ilyusha. All the participants give their consent to a solemn "Thou art", which is addressed to Ilyusha; and not to any particular aspect or act of his, but to Ilyusha in his original entirety, to Ilyusha in his deepest being. And thus they establish, communally and mutually, the original being, the independence and sacredness of each one of them— establish it not by detachment and fission from the Whole, but by means of the Whole.

It can be said with certainty that, so long as the

memory of Ilyusha remains alive in each of these children whom it has brought into a covenant together, it will preserve each of them from despair and collapse, from the final surrender to the spirit of not-being. Each of them will remember that in his early youth there was a scroll whose radiant lettering was clear and comprehensible to the pure and simple gaze of a child, what though in later years many of its characters may have become faded and blurred to a gaze blunted by life's sorrows. Each of them has made room within himself for the living presence of Ilyusha, as for something deeply native and constant, something inseparable from himself. In each of them he *is*, and he reminds each of them that it is possible to *be*, without sharing in the changeability of outward shows.

This experience of eternal memory brings with it the inward awareness of immortality. In each of these children the seed will germinate of faith in the union of all in the all-oneness of all, of faith in Christ who revealed Himself in the youthful and sole wealth of their hearts. And if these friends ever comprehend in its fullness the mystery of Christ, the signs of which are for the present revealed to them only in the features of their neighbour, then they will also understand that the covenant between them has its prototype in the Church: the Church as a community really and wholly bound together by the living person of Christ, and not by any abstract principle. They will understand that Christ himself has bound them together, through his martyr Ilyusha, and that their covenant signifies the communal glorification of the "Saint" of their small community.

4

When we pursue the hint concealed in the symbolic account of the establishment of this covenant, we arrive at the discovery of the principle governing what Dostoevsky declares to be Alyosha's "activity". He is to give the first impulse towards the realization of a true community of men of goodwill; a community maintained by mutual love in the name of Christ; a community whose aim is to bring the whole of life into the universal fold of the Church. When we recall that Alyosha intends to go and study at a university, we clearly see that he is carrying his mission to the Russia that has inwardly defected from the Church; to the Luciferian Russia whose search for the practical solution of social problems must lead, in Dostoevsky's view, primarily to a striving after the religious reinforcement and purification of human relationships.

When the active Luciferian principle encounters the active principle of Christ, the human vessel of the latter is subjected by Lucifer to a temptation after the pattern of the Temptation in the Wilderness. The active principle of the Kingdom of Heaven finds its earthly expression, and the act demanded seems thoroughly practicable and well-founded, provided only that the canons of Lucifer can be recognized as definitive. If, however, the human vessel of this active principle allows himself, whilst undergoing this temptation, to be led astray, and in his zeal for a practical realization to be betrayed into a compromise, then his endeavour will share the fate of all Luciferian efforts: whatever is achieved will prove to be unreal, a Will-o'-the-wisp, something without relation to the essence of things, despite the apparent tangibility of its forms.

The Name and the Figure of Christ—these are all that is given to the Christian "idea" on its way towards incarnation. There is for this "idea" no other principle, nor any other method of measurement. Yet all forms of civilization have been based on some principle outside the sphere of influence of this one figure. It follows, then, that no form of civilization, of any sort, is of itself serviceable for a construction of the new life in accordance with the "Christian idea".

This construction, therefore, will resemble—as is allegorically suggested in a Russian fairy-tale—a process of building the invisible Church with invisible bricks; and the artisans and architects themselves will be unable to perceive with their senses what they have erected until the invisible is revealed in glory. To those who are sent out to build in this World another World, and in this Kingdom another Kingdom, the behest is given: "That which is made, and will be made, upon earth and by men's laws, do not seek to destroy it; but your work is not governed by these laws."

Indeed, in so far as the Christian idea progressing towards fulfilment were to fail to penetrate, from within, the existing forms of civilization, and to subject them to the immanent tribunal of its blazing and all-consuming fire, in which they may either be melted and reshaped or else be burnt and fall to ashes like a mummy suddenly exposed to a breath of fresh air; or in so far as this idea were to attempt to clothe itself in any forms that civilization has hitherto created—to this extent it would become a part of this civilization, and would thereby annul and refute itself by the acceptance of a principle other than that of the living figure of Christ. It would prove itself to be but an association, dictated from without, amongst the existing associations of worldly factors; and whilst attempting to draw the world within the Church, it would itself immediately become secularized. In that case, however much the Church might dissociate itself from the State, it would inevitably end either in becoming an organ of the State or in "seeking to refashion itself into a State"—thus becoming subject to the diagnosis pronounced by Dostoevsky in his description of a process that, in his partisan judgment, is already occurring in western Christendom.[1] " Russian life and conceptions demand, not that the Church should pass, as from a lower into a higher type, into

---

[1] Dostoevsky's assertions concerning the transformation of the Catholic Church into a State; concerning the long-held intention of Christian Rome to complete the work of heathen Rome by a compulsory union of humanity in a theocratic, world-wide organization reminiscent of the Roman Empire; or concerning the betrayal of Christ by Popes who strove for earthly power, thus succumbing to the Second Temptation of Christ in the Wilderness and subjecting themselves, for the sake of world dominion, to the "wise and proud spirit": all these accusations, which Dostoevsky repeats with the passion of a fanatic, and which arise from an ancient prejudice, a terrified distrust of the *Ecclesia militans* and a credulous trust in its enemies, could be discussed only in a special critical survey, which would be scarcely appropriate in a work that sets out to describe Dostoevsky's positive religious ideals, but not his ecclesiastical polemics. It is, however, worth noting that neither the age-old subservience of the Eastern Church to the authority of the State, nor the incorporation of the Russian Church as an "ecclesiastical department" within the State organism, was regarded by Dostoevsky as being in any way a herald of the danger of a "transformation of Church into State"—although he fully recognizes the bare facts, as is shown by his statement that the Russian Church has been crippled since the time of Peter the Great. It is also worthy of mention that in his political essays, when he is discussing the possibility of an historical realization of his theocratic ideal, Dostoevsky expresses the view that the national Russian Church can develop into a "universal and all-powerful Church" only when the Russian nation has achieved a dominating position in the world, and, in particular, when it has gained control of Constantinople; whence it follows that he is setting up against Rome another Rome—a second Rome in Constantinople, and possibly a third Rome in Moscow. It should be added that this consent to the "Romish" attitude of mind is not put into the mouth of Father Zosima. Dostoevsky clearly did not succeed in harmonizing two contradictory conceptions concerning the development of his prophesied theocracy. On the one hand, he states that a particular political evolution must precede and regulate the realization of the theocratic ideal; and, on the other hand, he states (and this point of view is developed in *The Brothers Karamazov*) that the Kingdom of God grows in this world invisibly. According to this latter conception, the Kingdom transforms—quite independently of all earthly ways and means, and under the influence solely of divine grace—the whole structure of this world, and especially of the State, which it permits to become a Church.

the State; but, on the contrary, that the State should end by being worthy to become only the Church and nothing else. So be it! So be it!" ... "The Christian Church under Constantine entering into the State could, of course, surrender no part of its principles—the rock on which it stands—and could pursue no other aims than those which have been ordained and revealed by God himself, and among them that of drawing the whole world, and therefore the ancient pagan State itself, into the Church."

According, therefore, to the opinion of the monks of Zosima's circle, the Russian State must prove itself worthy to become, fully and in its entirety, that Church to which alone it is given "to have dominion on earth". It is significant that Ivan, who introduces the question of theocracy only quite timidly, and is therefore somewhat inclined towards a compromise with the State, says reassuringly: "All this will not degrade it in any way or take from it its honour and glory as a great State, nor from the glory of its rulers, but only turns it from a false, still pagan, mistaken path to the true and rightful path, which alone leads to the eternal goal."[1] The monks, however, who give final definition to this view of Ivan's, with which they are already familiar, do not repeat these reservations: they roundly reject all "compromises" and "agreements"; they make no promises whatsoever to the rulers who may happen to be in power during the period of transition from State to Church; and they are as silent concerning the form of the coming theocracy as they are clear and definite concerning its spirit.

How, in practice, can authority be exercised in a society that punishes crime only by excommunication? For such are the limits laid down by Father Zosima for the

---

[1] Translation from the Russian original by Constance Garnett.

powers of the ecclesiastical court which Ivan proposes should be the only court of law in the society of the future. It is scarcely to be wondered at that a liberal landowner who listens to the discussion is terrified by the monk's Utopianism.

Thus is shaped the "independent Russian idea" that determines Alyosha's mission in the world: the Russian communal being must become a truly religious communal being. The historical body of Russia must be zealous to become the body of a free theocracy: a theocracy so free that not even a court of law—that ultimate, most subtle and apparently so indispensable form of coercion—will be found there.

But, even if it were possible to realize this ideal on earth, how can preparations be made for its victory unless the Devil is driven out by the power of the Prince of Hell, unless coercion is fought with coercion, binding arrangements with other binding arrangements, historical forms by the creation of new forms on the same historical level, on the level of the same civilization?

When he who would do Christ's work has withstood the enticements of the Tempter, he feels himself at first, and until he has taken the first step, utterly poor and helpless, since he can find no earthly expression for his purpose nor any earthly means of carrying it out. Because he is "not of this world", he is in danger of proving to be not even of this earth, for whose very sake he has been sent into the world. He finds no place in human activity, and he has not where to lay his head. Father Zosima understands very well this initial perplexity of the chosen instrument; but he is not afraid of it, since he well knows that in a believer's heart it cannot turn into despondency.

"It is true," said Father Zosima, with a smile, "the

Christian society is not ready and is only resting on some seven righteous men, but as they are never lacking, it will continue still unshaken in expectation of its complete transformation from a society almost heathen in character, into a single universal and all-powerful Church. So be it, so be it. Even though at the end of the ages, for it is ordained to come to pass! And there is no need to be troubled about times and seasons, for the secret of the times and seasons is the wisdom of God, in His foresight, and in His love. And what in human reckoning seems far off, may, by Divine ordinance, be close at hand, on the eve of its appearance. And so be it, so be it!"[1]

5

Every abstract principle is, by reason of its negative nature, a principle of coercion. From such principles develop rules and normative concatenations. If the concrete—which can only incidentally be coercive—is to impose an obligation, it must first formulate itself as an abstract principle. Science is based on coercion no less than the State.

It is obvious that the union of human beings founded on Christ, that great concrete manifestation of Christian consciousness, is essentially alien to all the constructive efforts of civilization, which are invariably bound up with coercive decrees. This is the reason why religious truths have no compelling force of conviction for the intellect. It is true that within the Church, as a divine institution, there are law and order, obedience and hierarchy of a special sort; but these will be regarded as abstract principles only by one who remains spiritually alien to the Christian fellowship.

---

[1]Translation from the Russian original by Constance Garnett.

That which in popular speech is called "Holy Russia" has a certain concreteness without, however, being identified with the empirical data of the nation or of the State. Holy Russia means, however, not only what is holy in the nation—that, too, would be an abstraction—but is also a reverent and loving description of the concrete religious community which is founded on the concrete personality of Christ Himself, and persists to this day in the Russian homeland—or so it is popularly believed; and especially in the persons of the steadfastly enduring and loyal witnesses to Christ, his perennial Saints, those "seven righteous men" of whom Father Zosima says that Christian society rests upon them.

Holy Russia is the Russia of the holy treasures that the nation has received and enshrined in its heart, the Russia of the Saints, in whom and through whom these treasures have become incarnate and have sojourned among us. Holy Russia is also the broad territory that shares in this holiness, makes it a principle of its existence and sees in it the highest earthly good. It is the broad territory that in its ultimate depths remains loyal to its God-bearing focal point, and in this loyalty is forever united: not even sin can injure this unity, so long as the loyalty is unbroken. Holy Russia is, in short, all that is truly named Christian Orthodox Russia. In the people the concept of Catholicity is obscured by no tendency towards national isolation: of the Eastern Schism the people have in the main no knowledge.

It is to this spiritual unity of the people that Dostoevsky (although himself consciously a schismatic) refers when he writes: "The Russian people is entire in its Orthodoxy. It is the people's only substance and only possession; for Orthodoxy is all. . . . He who does not understand Orthodoxy will never have the slightest comprehension of the people. Nay, more—he cannot love the Russian people."

The sign of a true inner kinship with Holy Russia is the love of holiness, the acknowledgment that holiness is above all the crowns and glories of the world. Those who have lost touch with the people's sense of God may yet acknowledge holiness as a fixed value within the range of the highest spiritual values of humanity; but they will place many other achievements and possessions of mankind on at least as high a level, and will, indeed, certainly devote to these latter a far more lively and passionate love: to the lofty character, for example, that finds its consummation in high self-sacrifice (in so far as the moral value of this can be opposed to, or abstracted from, religion); and especially to human genius.

By glorifying holiness above all else, Dostoevsky simultaneously acknowledges the fact of the mysterious transformation that turns man, while still on earth, into another and divine nature. He understands how incomparable is the joy of the people when on its earthly fields, amid the stunted stalks half-choked by weeds, a blade shoots up that is born in God as the precursor of the coming crop of a better humanity; like a Eucharistic stalk in which the Holy Ghost has invisibly transformed the Earth into the Sun, the grains of wheat into the body of the Lamb.

In Dostoevsky's view the creative revelations of the human spirit have a functional connection with that "spiritual activity" of holiness—an activity invisible to us—which directly binds the Earth to "other worlds". It might be argued from this that, for example, there could have been no Dante had there not previously been a St. Francis of Assisi; or that Russia could not have achieved the mighty unfolding of its creative potentialities

that took place in the last century, had not previously
Saint Seraphim lived in the hermitage of Sarov as a pure
vessel of radiant spirituality. From the Saints come
epoch-making impulses towards a higher consciousness:
they are, as it were, antennæ extending the earth's
perceptions into higher worlds, and nerves that transmit
the influence of these worlds to earth.

In a homily of Father Zosima we read: "God took
seed from different worlds and sowed them in earth,
and his garden grew up and everything came up that
would come up, but what grows lives and is alive only
through the feeling of its contact with other mysterious
worlds."[1] Thus, too, in the highest utterances of human
genius there is something of holiness; for in its growth,
and in the moments when its creative will is awaking,
the soul of genius opens up to such contacts, and becomes
receptive to the influences exercised by the powers of
the invisible world: the powers whose vessels on earth
are those great souls who, once they have been finally
set free by death from all fetters of a negative self-
determination of the personality, and have truly received
Christ into themselves, are honoured by the Church
as Saints.

The lively sense of the guiding participation of the
great dead in the life of the living is to be found in all
religions that have attached a mystic significance to the
rites of the dead. In Novalis this feeling is extremely
intense, and in Goethe, too, it sometimes flares up. In
their actions these transfigured spirits are no longer
negatively self-determining, as personalities acting, like
us, of themselves and for themselves. On the contrary,
their self-determination is now positive, in that in their
works they identify themselves with the person who

[1]Translation from the Russian original by Constance Garnett.

receives their inspiration. Like Lohengrin, they keep their names and origins secret from the soul to which they draw near as to a bride. They are the true fathers of our good deeds, whereas we on earth are the mothers who carry them under our hearts and in agony bring them to birth. Nevertheless, the deed is certainly the deed of him who performs it—just as a child is in truth the child of its mother—and yet it is not exclusively his deed. And the highest thing in human creative effort is the opening-up of the soul to the fructifying Word, as expressed in the saying: "Behold, the handmaid of the Lord!"

In *The Brothers Karamazov* is it not Zosima, by this time already deceased, who at the decisive moment restrains Dimitri from parricide? "My story, gentlemen?" said Dimitri at the preliminary hearing. "Well, it was like this: whether it was someone's tears, or my mother prayed to God, or a good angel kissed me at that instant, I don't know. But the devil was conquered."[1] This kiss from beyond the grave is, in Dostoevsky's conception, the complement to Zosima's genuflexion before Dimitri in the cell, the genuflexion that foretold to Dimitri the expiatory suffering in store for him. And is it not this same Zosima who "visits" Alyosha's soul in that decisive hour when he "had fallen on the earth a weak boy, and rose up a resolute champion".[1]

Since communion with the dead is an essential component of the mystical life of the Christian fellowship, the above considerations clearly show us the deep religious meaning of the covenant made in everlasting memory of Ilyusha.

---

[1] Translation from the Russian original by Constance Garnett.

6

The acknowledgment of holiness as the highest value is the foundation of the people's philosophy of life, and the symbol of the people's longing for Holy Russia. "Orthodoxy", then, is precisely the state of universal unification with the sanctuary and of all-oneness with the Saints. Dostoevsky repeatedly mentions the widespread belief, which he has observed in the people, that the Earth continues to exist only in virtue of the fact that her holiness never fails; that somewhere, in the desert, in inaccessible wastes, are a few holy men. The Orthodox world, the world of the Russian Faith, extends in circles about this mysteriously scattered brotherhood; and therefore, however black the periphery of this Orthodox world, its spiritual life is fed by the vitalizing stream—the stream, as it were, of the blood of Christ himself—that flows from this centre, from this heart that burns with devotion and longs "with an ineffable longing" for the Holy Ghost. He who severs himself from the spiritual Communion of Saints severs himself also from Orthodoxy; and, conversely, he who rejects Orthodoxy abandons also the Saints.

Orthodoxy is the citadel of Holy Russia, which is erected, with foundations deep in the national faith, against the might of Ahriman. This citadel is indestructible and impregnable; but its battle for the earth against the Princes of this World is not yet over. The foe, however, is weakened by inner discord; and the house or the State that is divided against itself will not stand. The dynamism of Lucifer drives Ahriman from his sphere of influence; although, to be sure, this is not final, and is more a matter of appearance than of actuality. Lucifer destroys and disperses the manifestations of

Ahriman's self-assertion, and Ahriman must once more, and by new methods, reconquer his lost territories: just as mildew that has been removed from a surface at once again starts invading it, as long as the surrounding atmosphere is not changed. (This, by the way, is the reason why Dostoevsky arrives at a positive evaluation of the achievement of Peter the Great.)

Immediately around the citadel, however, lies the ring of the beleaguering hosts of Ahriman. Daemons are attracted by what is holy, they prowl around it like jackals, and the ravings of Father Therapont, Zosima's opponent, who exclaims that devils swarm around Zosima, are the ravings of a clairvoyant who does not understand what he sees. Zosima himself is prepared to give these spirits of Not-being anything to which they are in any degree entitled. But their cry is: "corruption to the corruptible!" And there is a close connection between the mystery of the division of the personality into the corruptible and the incorruptible, the transient and the permanent—the mystery of the death of the sown seed, without which death it cannot spring up and bear fruit—and the deep and cruel symbolism of the "smell of corruption".

The Brothers Karamazov is a prophecy that the Russia of the future will present the spiritual drama of a relationship between the three Powers that will be different from any relationship hitherto known. Holy Russia will not allow the besieging darkness of Ahriman to sweep over her; not only will Ahriman's triumph be swept away by the dynamism of the Luciferian Russia, as the fancies of winter are swept away by the hot sunshine of the brief northern summer; but Holy Russia will herself send out her champions into the midst of the civilization dominated by Lucifer, and will permeate

HAGIOLOGY

it with the invisible rays of a Thebaid that works by
stealth.

Dostoevsky never went so far as to foretell how all
this will be accomplished; but he has predicted what
must occur. *The Brothers Karamazov* treats of "the
mission of the Russian monk"; but by monasticism
Dostóevsky understands primarily a new, mystical
monastic consecration, an ascetism, discipline and
readiness to serve in the world that will be disclosed by
no outward insignia. These anonymous monks and lay
brothers will be sent out into the fields of humanity, not
to weed out the tares, which must, as Christ says, grow
up with the corn, but to be as the warmth of the sun and
a quickening rain coming in due season.

The whole life of Russia must be permeated by a
principle quite different from the principles that have
hitherto governed the organization of life. Once it is
permeated by this new principle, all forms of coercion
and constraint, and of the organized lie, will fall to
pieces—some all of a sudden, others in slow and gradual
disintegration, one after another; whilst the forms that
are capable of containing the principle of Christ will
undergo a transformation and achieve an undreamed-of
fluorescence: the rose-hip will itself become the rose.
The Christian universal unity is not possible without a
common object of love—an object alive, because only
what is alive can be loved. What though the principles
upon which a deed is founded be all-uniting, all-affirming,
all-human, they do not warrant an action that truly frees
and unites men if they are not built upon the love of
Christ. For a Christian, the good and the bad are determined by the image of Christ living in his soul. Even
among the people dwelling together in mutual and daily
intercourse, those alone can be essentially bound by

Christ who realize Him as a Person; those alone are genuinely good who genuinely love Him. Only such a bond does not diminish the personality but strengthens it.

God knows who really loves Him and who does not. There is a deep significance, which applies to all modes of human action, in the Gospel story of the two men who do the same earthly work, and of whom one is chosen and the other rejected. This is also what happens to the two who work together, and are both alike acknowledged, as liberators: but the one is truly engaged in the task of liberation, whilst the other is forging the chains of slavery; and of the two, who are both alike acknowledged as builders, the one is building and the other is destroying.

The Christian universal unity will be an invisible and all-embracing unification of a divided and far-scattered stock. It will be the consciousness, awaking the action and growing in strength, of the real unity of men; of that unity to which Luciferian civilization opposes the treacherous mirages of manifold combinations based on abstract principles. This universal unity—to which nothing is given, that it may prevail over the world, save the One Name and the One Figure—displays, so Dostoevsky believes, to the inward vision a perfect co-ordination of its living parts and a profoundly harmonious structure. From the mark of its inner structure it may be called Hagiocracy, government by the Saints.

Hagiocracy is already preparing the way for the "free Theocracy"[1]; the way for the longingly awaited future of the reign of Christ over men.

---

[1] To quote an expression used by the man who was Dostoevsky's young friend and fellow-pilgrim during the years when our author was frequenting the society of monks and priests and was studying Russian mysticism and asceticism—by the great Vladimir Solovyev.

Fall = defection from divine
where is the divine — inside you

hence fall = defection
from self — self-division

All deities reside in the
human breast